Friedrich Ebert

Makers
of the
Modern
World

Friedrich Ebert
Germany
Harry Harmer

HAUS HISTORIES

First published in Great Britain in 2008 by
Haus Publishing Ltd
26 Cadogan Court
Draycott Avenue
London SW3 3BX
www.hauspublishing.com

A CIP catalogue record for this book
is available from the British Library

ISBN 978-1-905791-63-7

Series design by Susan Buchanan
Typeset in Sabon by MacGuru Ltd
Printed in Dubai by Oriental Press
Maps by Martin Lubikowski, ML Design, London

Contents

The German delegation awaits presentation of draft Versailles treaty, May 1919. Prussian Assembly President Robert Leinert, finance specialist Theodor Melchior, Posts Minister Johannes Giesberts, Foreign Minister Ulrich von Brockdorff-Rantzau, Justice Minister Otto Landsberg, and international law specialist Walter Schuecking.

The enemy's revengeful hysteria

The German delegation reacted to the peace proposals presented at Versailles on 7 May 1919 with a combination of disbelief and outrage. A copy of the bulky draft treaty before him, the delegation's leader, Foreign Minister Count Ulrich von Brockdorff-Rantzau, told the world's peacemakers gathered in the Trianon Palace, 'We are aware that the strength of German arms has been crushed. We can feel all the power of hate we must encounter in this assembly ... It is demanded of us that we admit ourselves the only parties guilty of this war – on my lips such an admission would be a lie.'[1]

Georges Clemenceau, the French prime minister and chairman of the Peace Conference, had left the Germans in no doubt about the victors' attitude in his brusque opening speech. 'This is neither the time nor the place for superfluous words. You have before you the accredited plenipotentiaries of the greater and lesser Powers, both Allied and Associated, that for four years have carried on without respite the merciless war which has been imposed upon them. The time has come for a heavy reckoning of accounts. You have asked for peace. We are prepared to offer you peace.'[2] There would be no face-to-face negotiations, though the Allies and Associated powers (hereafter, the Allies) would accept written comments on the draft. Germany was given two weeks to digest and comment on the treaty's 440 articles, some 80,000 words covering over 200 pages.

By the terms of the treaty, Germany was to lose almost a tenth of her population, 25,000 square miles of territory in Europe to her neighbours, and her African and Asian colonies. To ensure that Germany would not emerge from the war larger than she had entered it in 1914, union with what remained of the diminished Austrian Empire was forbidden. The army was to be limited to 100,000 men, conscription would be abolished, no air force permitted and the navy severely restricted. Germany would pay reparations for the damage she and her allies had caused in the war, the precise amount to be determined by May 1921. Articles 227–231 caused the greatest uproar in Germany. The former Kaiser and military advisors accused of war crimes were to be handed over to the Allies for trial and Germany was to acknowledge her responsibility for the war.

After a hurried translation and scrutiny of the draft treaty, Brockdorff-Rantzau complained to Clemenceau on 9 May that some demands were intolerable, while others were impossible to comply with. On the same day Germany's provisional Reich President, Friedrich Ebert, accused the Allies of abandoning their promise that President Woodrow Wilson's Fourteen Points would form the basis of what Germany had believed would be a just settlement. *From such an imposed peace fresh hatred would be bound to arise between the nations, and in the course of history there would be new wars ... The dismemberment and mangling of the German Nation, the delivering of German labour to foreign capitalism for the indignity of wage slavery, and the permanent fettering of the young German republic by the Entente's imperialism is the aim of this peace of violence ... In view of this danger of destruction, the German nation and the Government which it chose must stand by each other, knowing no parties.*[3] The entire sweep of the German press – liberal, socialist, conservative and nationalist – echoed his sentiments. Cardinal Hartmann, the Archbishop of Cologne, appealed to the Pope to intervene and prevent what he described as a cruel imposition that would utterly ruin Germany.

The German Chancellor Philipp Scheidemann condemned the treaty in the National Assembly in Berlin on 12 May. Pointing to the document before him he said, 'I ask you: who can, as an honest man, I will not say as a German, but only as an honest, straightforward man, accept such terms? What hand would not wither that binds itself and us in these fetters?'[4] Speakers for each of the parties rose to echo Scheidemann. The Social Democrat

> **'What hand would not wither that binds itself and us in these fetters?'**
> SCHEIDEMANN, 12 MAY 1919

Heinrich Müller described the treaty as intolerable and said it could not, in any case, be fulfilled. Only Hugo Haase, leader of the Independent Socialists who had broken from the Social Democrats, argued that Germany should sign – on the basis that the treaty would be made irrelevant by the revolution he believed was sweeping the world.

Addressing a large demonstration at the Lustgarten in Berlin, Ebert said Germany could not accept the treaty as it stood, *the product of the enemy's revengeful hysteria.*[5] The cabinet – made up of representatives of the Social Democrats, the Catholic Centre Party and the Democrats – issued a statement on 20 May: 'Germany declines to sign the peace terms laid before it because they spell the economic destruction, political dishonour, and moral degradation of the entire German nation, not only for the present, but also for still unborn generations.' Matthias Erzberger, the Centre Party's leader, warned an American intelligence officer in Berlin that Ebert had told him *I am not so sure that we won't fight when the time comes* because he found the terms so repugnant.[6]

Brockdorff-Rantzau despatched Germany's voluminous, detailed, but ultimately fruitless counterproposals to Clemenceau on 29 May. In their reply on 16 June, the Allies left the thrust of the treaty unchanged, granting only minor concessions on Germany's borders with the new Polish state. Germany was given five days to accept or reject the terms, with the clear implication that rejection meant a renewal of the war. The German delegation arrived at Weimar, where the government was now sitting, on 18 June. Brockdorff-Rantzau advised the cabinet that the delegation considered the treaty unacceptable. Discussion among the ministers, chaired by President Ebert, continued until 3 o'clock the following morning. The cabinet had also to consider advice from the army commander, Field Marshal Paul von Hindenburg. What he said was carefully ambiguous: the army would be unable to resist a renewed advance by the overwhelming might of the British, French and American armies. 'A favourable outcome of our operations is therefore very doubtful, but as a soldier I would rather perish in honour than sign a humiliating peace.'[7] The cabinet divided, six in favour of signing, eight – including Chancellor Scheidemann – against. Ebert said that without a cabinet consensus, the National Assembly would have to make the final decision.

The divisions in the cabinet reflected uncertainties in the parties that made up the coalition. In separate meetings on

20 June the Democrats voted unanimously against signing, the Social Democrats 75 for and 35 against, while a majority of the Centre Party favoured acceptance provided the Allies removed the articles on war guilt and war crimes. Scheidemann went directly from the Social Democrats' meeting to Ebert's office, accompanied by Otto Landsberg, Minister of Justice and a member of the deputation at Versailles. Both told him they were resigning. Ebert asked them to stay. When they refused, a despairing Ebert – who in May had publicly proclaimed Germany's determination to reject the treaty – said he must also give up his office. They persuaded him to remain, arguing that his resignation would leave Germany in chaos. A little later Brockdorff-Rantzau announced that the Versailles delegation would be standing down.

Three days before the Allied ultimatum for signature was due to expire Germany had no government and no delegation to the Peace Conference. On 22 June, with one day remaining, the Social Democrat Gustav Bauer formed a new coalition with the Centre. His administration's first task, Bauer said, would be to conclude what he called 'this peace of injustice'. Later that day he presented a resolution to the National Assembly: 'The government of the German republic is ready to sign the peace treaty without thereby acknowledging that the German people are the responsible authors of the war and without accepting Articles 227 to 231.'[8] After three hours of debate the deputies voted 237 to 138 in favour of the resolution.

The government telegraphed the National Assembly's decision to Clemenceau who replied at 9 p.m. 'The Allied and Associated Powers feel constrained to say that the time for discussion is past. They can accept or acknowledge no qualification or reservation ...'[9] Germany was to communicate her rejection or acceptance of the treaty as it stood by 7 p.m on 23 June. With no remaining room for manoeuvre, Ebert sought the army command's final opinion on whether Germany had the capability to resist, to re-open the bloody conflict that had ravaged Europe.

Top: Friedrich Ebert with his family, summer 1916
Bottom: The Ebert children (from the left): Heinrich (falls in the war), Georg (falls in the war), Fritz (is wounded), Amalie, and Karl

I

The Life and the Land

Leaders of the Social Democratic Party, Leipzig 1909
Back row, from the left: Luise Zietz, Friedrich Ebert, Hermann Müller,
Robert Wengels
Front row, from the left: Alwin Gerisch, Paul Singer, August Bebel,
Wilhem Pfannkuch, Hermann Molkenbuhr

1

The Party Man, 1871–1913

Friedrich Ebert's life was entwined with the birth and the death of the German Empire. On 18 January 1871 Wilhelm I of Prussia was proclaimed German Emperor in the Hall of Mirrors at Versailles in a ceremony intended to humiliate a France recently defeated in war. On 4 February 1871 Ebert was born in Heidelberg into a tradesman's family. At the age of 48, he succeeded the last Hohenzollern Emperor, Wilhelm II, as the head of the German state, the first commoner to hold that position. Ebert's father, Karl, was a master tailor, successful, relatively prosperous, a Roman Catholic with socialist sympathies. His mother, Katharina, was a Protestant and bore nine children, of which Ebert was the seventh. The writer Mark Twain, visiting Heidelberg during Ebert's boyhood, described in *A Tramp Abroad* the beauty of the town, perched on the river Necker, dominated by a picturesque ruined castle, students from Europe and America thronging the ancient university.

Ebert had an elementary education, leaving his Catholic school at 14, but showed some academic potential. A local priest tried to persuade the family to put him forward for the church, opening the opportunity to more advanced education. Ebert may have argued that he lacked spiritual devotion, though he retained a lifelong sympathy for Catholicism despite the free-thinking nature of the party in which he made his career. He became an apprentice saddle maker in 1885 and completed his induction into the leather-working trade – based in small workshops rather than the factories spreading across a rapidly industrialising Germany – towards the end of 1888. As a child Ebert's friends had seen him as mischievous; as an apprentice this became rebelliousness, a trait that faded as responsibility revealed a conformist personality and a rigid mind.

Mocked more than once in later life for his original trade – the Weimar Republic's right-wing press described him as the 'saddler-President' – Ebert's touchy response was to say this was as absurd as calling a general a lieutenant because he had once held that rank. He contained within himself the conflicts of the new Germany with its Catholic south, Protestant north and growing industrial working class. Otto von Bismarck, the Prussian architect of unification, had turned first against the Catholics and then against the socialists, fearing that both had loyalties beyond the state he was constructing – the Catholics to Rome, the socialists to Marxist internationalism. Ebert, who was born a Catholic and became a socialist, straddled the Empire's 'outsider' groups.

Germany's first significant working-class party – the Socialist Workers' Party of Germany (SAPD) – was established in 1875. Three years later, following two assassination attempts on Kaiser Wilhelm I, allegedly by socialists, Bismarck, now Imperial Chancellor, banned the SAPD from organising, exiling the party's most prominent activists and theoreticians. He placed no obstacle in the way of Socialists contesting for seats in the Reichstag, which, though elected, was impotent.

Bismarck had also feared a working class and liberal middle class alliance that would press for parliamentary democracy.

The ban – which extended to socialist trade unions – was to last until 1890. It was, therefore, an underground party that Ebert joined in 1889, encouraged by an uncle in Mannheim. His apprenticeship complete, Ebert began seeking work as a journeyman – the first stage towards the status of self-employed master – at the same time joining the saddle makers' union. He moved between Brunswick, Frankfurt, Hersfeld, Kassel and Hanover, taking what work he could find, meanwhile organising, building a reputation from town to town among the predominantly skilled workers attracted to trade-unionism and then to socialist politics. Ebert's commitment and competence as an activist stood out and in 1890 he was elected secretary of the union federation in Hanover.

Still in his teens, Ebert had found the role he was to make his own, culminating with his arrival at the summit of the German state. He was prepared to carry out the organisational routines few were keen to undertake, acting as the negotiator and master of detail, the puller of strings. But in conditions of illegality and in the economic recession of the early 1890s, Ebert was frequently unemployed, watched by the police and blacklisted by employers. He read widely, Marx and Engels of course, but also Owen and Lassalle. One historian has written: 'He became convinced that there was no hope for the future of the working classes in a pure capitalistic system.' [1] The party's theoreticians, exiled and with a sense of persecution, took on a more radical cast, using the word 'revolution' freely. But, as Karl Kautsky – the 'Pope of Marxism' – was to write: 'It is not a question of a revolution in the sense in which the police use the word, that is to say of an armed revolt.' [2]

Europe 1914

Petrograd (St Petersburg)

Riga

Moscow

Vilna

Königsberg

RUSSIAN EMPIRE

Warsaw   Brest-Litovsk

Kiev

Budapest

RY   Odessa

ROMANIA

Belgrade   Bucharest   *Black Sea*

SERBIA   BULGARIA

Sofia

NIA   Constantinople

GREECE   **OTTOMAN EMPIRE**

Athens

Bismarck complicated matters by instituting a paternalistic welfare state, attempting to bribe the working class into docility with pensions, accident insurance and unemployment benefits, rudimentary but an advance on anything Germany's European neighbours had achieved. When, after dismissing Bismarck in 1890, the newly enthroned Kaiser Wilhelm II lifted the ban on socialist parties in an attempt to win the workers' affection, the party re-emerged as the German Social Democratic Party (Sozialdemokratische Partei Deutschlands – SPD). The self-proclaimed Marxist SPD's 1891 Erfurt Programme set out 'maximum' and 'minimum' demands – the maximum looking confidently to capitalism's inevitable and even imminent collapse (making the party prone to a comfortable fatalism); the minimum seeking a range of reforms including genuine parliamentary democracy, a thoroughgoing welfare state financed through direct taxation, and the eight-hour working day. The SPD fell into the paradox that haunted its history – radical rhetoric masking reformist practice, the contradiction between the two carefully evaded until brought sharply into focus by war and revolution, with Ebert playing a central part.

ooooo

Ebert's travels brought him in May 1891 to the North German city of Bremen, a port on the river Weser, where he remained for 15 years. Bremen combined a captivating attractiveness with a staunch sense of local autonomy. In 1871 the city's population had been a little over 80,000; when Ebert left this had soared to almost a quarter of a million, boosted by industrialisation. In 1878 there had been fewer than 6,000 workers in Bremen's manufacturing sector; within 20 years their number would rise almost six-fold, with an accompanying increase in SPD membership.

Ebert made efforts to establish himself as an independent craftsman, with little success. Taking whatever casual opening was available, he lived precariously, combining work with trade union and SPD activism. He agitated for the democratisation of Bremen's local government, while at the same time pressing for centralisation of the trade union and SPD machinery. His position accorded precisely with that of the skilled workers becoming unionised and joining the now legal SPD, seeking to improve their status and conditions in a capitalist state rather than acting as shock troops to topple it.

In 1893 Ebert married Louise Rump, a working-class woman who shared his politics. Ebert's lifelong friend Hermann Müller (they first became acquainted in the Bremen SPD) believed a settled family life made Ebert more conciliatory in nature, giving his politics a firmer foundation. The couple's first child, also called Friedrich, was born in September 1894. They were to have in all one daughter, Amalie, and four sons, two of whom were killed in the First World War, both in 1917. *I have lost two sons for this Empire*, Ebert told the Imperial Chancellor in 1918 when the latter questioned his commitment.[3] Friedrich junior was wounded.

Ebert's politics notwithstanding, he had a working relationship with Bremen's capitalists. Towards the end of 1893 negotiations with the owners of a local brewery, Beck's, concluded with Ebert becoming an innkeeper, the brewers setting him up in business in return for a guaranteed outlet for their beer. A socialist landlord could count on socialist and trade union customers. As the SPD renewed its organisation and recruitment, the *parteikneipe* (party tavern or pub) served as both a social and political centre. Ebert's wife and mother-in-law helped with the day-to-day running of the business. The 'hail fellow well met' aspect of inn keeping was not to Ebert's taste, his wife reputedly reproaching him on one occasion, 'As a host you should not look like a vinegar merchant who has had to drink his own vinegar'.[4]

Ebert soon transformed the inn into the Bremen SPD headquarters, placing himself at the centre of the city's party and trade union activity. Now 22 and freed from the uncertainty of an existence as an employee, Ebert matured as an administrator – energetic and unfailingly precise – and as a speaker. Though never

> 'As a host you should not look like a vinegar merchant who has to drink his own vinegar.'
>
> LOUISE EBERT

an inspiring orator (like Rosa Luxemburg), or a sophisticated Marxist wordspinner (like Karl Kautsky), what Ebert said carried the weight of his organising experience. His election as local party chairman in 1894 marked the beginning of his rise to power nationally. In the same year Ebert became editor of the SPD city paper, the *Bremer-Bürgerzeitung*, a post paying 25 marks a week and which he held for six years. Ebert's reputation grew with his appearance as a delegate at the 1896 Gotha national congress and his election as an SPD member on the Bremen city council in 1899. In 1900 he became party leader on the council and the city's first paid labour secretary, holding trade union activity throughout the city together, advising members on employment rights, intimately involved with their everyday lives.

Ebert's rise in the Bremen party coincided with the country's transition from an agricultural to an industrial economy, with an expansion that would enable Germany to challenge then outstrip her nearest European rival, Britain. Germany's population rose from 41 million in 1871 to 68 million in 1913. As a latecomer to industrialisation, Germany was not – unlike Britain – encumbered with outdated techniques and combined an efficient and rigorous educational system with scientific and financial innovation. German iron and steel output rose from 4.1 million tons in 1880 to 6.3 million in 1900 and soared to 17.6 million in 1913. By comparison, British production fell from 8 million tons in 1880 to 5 million in 1900, rising only to 7.7 million in 1913. German steel production in 1913 exceeded that of Britain, Russia and France combined. Germany was second to none in the production of electrical, chemical and pharmaceutical goods. In the first decade of the 20th century Germany's exports rose by over 90 per cent, Britain's by only 75 per cent, and by 1913 German sales abroad almost equalled those of Britain. If France shuddered at the military implications of her neighbour's soaring population and impatient energy, Britain eyed warily Germany's burgeoning industrial power and naval ambitions.

The new Germany was a contradictory but dynamic combination of absolutism and democracy. In 1875 Marx had pointedly portrayed Bismarck's creation as a 'bureaucratically constructed military despotism, dressed up with parliamentary forms, mixed in with an element of feudalism yet at the same time already influenced by the bourgeoisie'.[5] Every day the working class was left in no doubt that it lay outside society, discriminated against in the electoral system of the states making up Germany, particularly in the largest, Prussia. Compulsory military service – with militarism the glue holding the nation together – heightened the sense of a tight hierarchical order (the officer corps saw the barracks as the 'school of the nation') but confirmed a nagging class-consciousness. The Kaiser's earlier sympathy for the proletariat having waned, during a Berlin tramworkers' strike in 1900 he blustered, 'I expect, if the troops are called out, at least five hundred people to bite the dust.'[6]

The paradox for Ebert's party was that while delegates to annual congresses traditionally declared a theoretical enmity to capitalism, confident that the system was inevitably doomed, capitalism – despite periodic crises – was thriving and creating a prosperous industrial working class. Wages were rising and a substantial section of the workforce, particularly the skilled who were the mainstay of SPD membership, saw real improvements in their standard of living. Income per capita doubled in Germany between 1870 and 1913. How could this be reconciled with the party's conviction that workers' conditions would worsen, that capitalism would collapse and socialism would emerge? The party's membership rose from an estimated 100,000 in 1890 to almost 400,000 in 1904 and over a million in 1914. The growth mirrored the steady increase in SPD votes in elections to the Reichstag – from 312,000 in 1881, to 1,427,000 in 1890, and to over three million in 1903.

A party theoretician, Eduard Bernstein, suggested in the late 1890s that Marx had been mistaken, that capitalism was not about to disintegrate, that its crises were manageable, and that the SPD's objectives required revision. Calling the party programme into question, he wrote, 'I frankly admit that I have extraordinarily little feeling for, or interest in, what is usually called "the final goal of socialism". This goal, whatever it may be, is nothing to me; but the movement is everything.'[7] Bernstein considered the SPD would achieve more by working with bourgeois liberals to create a genuine parliamentary democracy. Passing one good factory law, he once said, might contribute more to the workers' welfare than nationalising an entire industry. The party was riven with bitter debates and Bernstein's revisionism was rejected at party congresses in favour of radical rhetoric. Ebert kept his distance from the revisionists but shared their views in practice, declaring in 1901, *A state can work in the interest of the general good only if it gives an opportunity to all classes of the populace to participate in governing, in administering, and in developing the state.*[8] The party's task was to find a place for the working class in the Imperial state, not overthrow it.

ooooo

August Bebel, the party's leader since 1875, regarded Ebert as too moderate for his orthodox Marxist taste in 1904 and blocked an advance in his career. Ebert presided over that year's SPD congress in Bremen. Bebel's co-chairman, Paul Singer, was impressed with Ebert's conduct of the congress, recommending his selection as a paid official. Bebel vetoed this. But a year later he relented and the party delegates confirmed Ebert's appointment as a secretary on the executive. Reformist trade union leaders were prominent in Ebert's support, confident that he would provide organisational ability and dogged reliability to an SPD transforming itself from an agitational faction to an electoral machine.

> 'A short fat man, with short legs, a short neck, and a pear-shaped head on a pear-shaped body.'
> **SEBASTIAN HAFFNER ON FRIEDRICH EBERT**

The SPD executive was made up of two co-chairmen – Bebel and Singer – a treasurer and four secretaries. One historian of the SPD describes the new recruit to the party leadership: 'Colorless, cool, determined, industrious, and intensely practical, Ebert had all those characteristics which were to make of him, *mutatis mutandis*, the Stalin of Social Democracy.'[9] This is unfair. Ebert may have shared Stalin's preference for administration over idealism, but not his personal cruelty. Stalin wrote poetry and robbed a bank in his early life; it is hard to imagine Ebert contemplating either. His hair still black, the 35-year-old Ebert's appearance contrasted sharply with that of the older generation of SPD leaders. An unsympathetic writer describes him, unflatteringly but accurately, as a 'short fat man, with short legs, a short neck, and a pear-shaped head on a pear-shaped body'.[10]

Ebert arrived at the Berlin headquarters early in 1906 to discover ramshackle offices and casual administrative practices more appropriate to the SPD's origins as a sect than the major political force it aspired to be. Party reforms agreed over the previous two years made it clear that the SPD saw its future in the Reichstag rather than in the streets, with a tiered structure based on electoral constituencies. Ebert's personality and talents ensured those reforms would be rigorously pursued. He was initially deputed to assist the treasurer, the ageing revisionist Karl Gerish, in collating membership statistics and subscription records. The office had no typewriter, no telephone and no clerical assistance, deficiencies Ebert made good within a year. He formalised an organisational hierarchy, using to the full the party's new insistence on regular and detailed written reports from regional and constituency officials, gnawing away at local autonomy.

The party's radical wing had hoped that a tighter, more centralised organisation would thwart the revisionist heresy. In practice, the bureaucracy – which sought stability above all – served the interests of moderates and reformers. Within a few years of Ebert's arrival on the executive, the rapidly-growing party had over 4,000 paid officials and a further

11,000 salaried employees. The contemporary German social theorist Max Weber would cite Ebert as a prime example of the political bureaucrat, the ambitious functionary of a state within a state. Heinrich Müller, who soon joined his friend Ebert on the executive, once boasted that he had never read Marx's *Das Kapital*. Many, though not Ebert, could probably have said the same. Radical thoughts might lead to radical action, which would invite government repression and threaten the survival of the organisation and the individual bureaucrat's personal advancement. Better to construct a majority in the Reichstag through patient practical work. But Germany's half-built democracy had a sense of unreality. The people might elect their representatives, but not their rulers. As Eric Hobsbawm has written: 'The SPD did not practice politics, but merely waited (in theory) until historic inevitability brought it an electoral majority and hence "the revolution", while concealing (in practice) a subaltern acceptance of the status quo by providing its members with a large collective private world.'[11]

Ebert could at least ensure the machine worked smoothly. In the decade after his appointment to the executive, the SPD constructed a network of social and sports clubs, expanded women's and youth groups and established a school in Berlin to broaden the political education of party and trade union officials. By 1914 the party had over 90 daily newspapers in towns and cities throughout the country, while the investment of 20 million marks of party funds yielded a substantial financial return. The SPD became the world's largest workers' party, admired for the efficiency of its organisation and what appeared its dedication to the transformation of society. There was a hint of militancy in Ebert's supervision of the growing party youth movement, where he worked amicably with the radical Karl Liebknecht. But Rosa Luxemburg, the SPD's most colourful and influential revolutionary, complained to a friend, 'German party life is nothing but a bad dream, or rather a dreamless leaden sleep.' [12]

The 1905 Russian Revolution, combined with economic setbacks in Germany, triggered a wave of enthusiasm among the party's rank and file and that year's congress adopted a resolution supporting the use of mass strikes to defend the right to vote. At the Mannheim congress the following year, Bebel sought to set the government's mind at rest by making it clear the SPD would not resort to a general strike to prevent Germany becoming involved in a European war, denouncing the notion as 'childish'. He believed the masses would not support such action and that the government would impose a state of emergency and arrest the party's leaders. The 1907 elections to the Reichstag showed the danger to the SPD of inviting the government to paint it as unpatriotic.

The January 1907 elections took place against the background of mounting antagonism between the European powers. The Naval Bills of 1898 and 1900 had demonstrated Wilhelm II's ambition to build a fleet that would rival the British navy and press Germany's self-assertive *Weltpolitik*. A Triple Alliance of Germany, Austria-Hungary and Italy (formed in 1882) faced the Triple Entente that had grown from the Franco-Russian military pact of 1894 and the Anglo-French *entente cordiale* of 1904, consolidated by the Anglo-Russian agreement in 1907. In March 1905 the Kaiser made a maladroit speech in Tangier, attempting to thwart France's Moroccan ambitions and split the Anglo-French *entente*. France, backed by Britain, moved troops to the frontier and Germany mobilised reserves. An international conference at Algeçiras averted a clash, but tension remained. The

Schlieffen Plan, formulated by the German chief of staff in 1905, assumed that Germany would fight a future war on two fronts, against France and Russia. A German radical socialist had remarked perceptively in 1899 that with colonial expansion having reached its limit, 'The European powers will have no choice other than throwing themselves on one another, until the period of the final crisis sets in within politics.' [13]

In 1897 Bernhard von Bülow, as Foreign Minister, had demanded that Germany should seize her rightful 'place in the sun'. Now, in 1907, as Imperial Chancellor, he mounted a rabidly nationalist election campaign. The SPD responded by condemning the government's military and colonial policies, in particular the brutal repression of a rising in German South West Africa, enabling right-wingers to arouse fears that Germany was threatened externally by envious rivals and internally by unpatriotic socialists. The SPD's representation in the Reichstag slumped from 83 seats to 43. The results were a personal disappointment to Ebert, who failed to win a seat

WILHELM II (1859–1941)
A grandson of Queen Victoria, Wilhelm succeeded his father as King of Prussia and German Emperor (or Kaiser) in 1888 and asserted his new course by dismissing Bismarck, the architect of national unity, in 1890. Wilhelm had an emotional attachment to his armed forces and unsettled Europe with his unpredictable foreign policies and ambivalent feelings towards Britain. During the First World War he was nominally supreme commander but became a figurehead, eclipsed by the Hindenburg-Ludendorff 'silent dictatorship'. Reluctantly abdicating in November 1918, Wilhelm spent the remainder of his life on an estate in the Netherlands. He wrote two uninformative volumes of memoirs.

he had expected to take in Hanover. They also undermined party confidence, calling into question the inevitable electoral advance it had always assumed.

The right-wing SPD deputy Gustav Noske summed up a view that the party's interests were better served by flowing with the nationalist tide than by embracing radicalism. He told the Reichstag that the SPD would not allow foreign states to intimidate Germany and that military disarmament was for a future socialist society, not for the present. How close the 1905 Moroccan crisis had come to igniting a European conflict prompted the Socialist International to clarify its attitude towards war. At the International's congress in Stuttgart in 1907 French delegates called for a general strike by the workers of every country to prevent war. Bebel, the SPD leader, disagreed, saying that the patriotism of the working class could not be ignored. A final compromise resolution advocated that Socialist parties should do all in their power to prevent the outbreak of war. 'Should, however, war break out, the parties are obliged, while working for its speedy termination, to use the ensuing upheaval to arouse the people and thus to precipitate the downfall of capitalist class rule.' [14] As was usually the case with the International's proclamations, there was nothing to say how this would be achieved.

ooooo

Ebert saw the SPD's electoral setback in organisational rather than ideological terms. At the party congress following the 1907 elections his analysis was rigorously practical. He boasted of the rising number of regional secretaries, but complained that 150 local parties had ignored his request for information to include in the annual report. He told delegates he was striving for uniform management of the party's affairs and that they should now have their eyes set on the 1912 Reichstag elections. Ebert worked to consolidate his own and the SPD's relationship with the financially powerful trade union leaders, moderates who increasingly dominated the party's tone, ensuring it was a labour rather than a socialist movement. Ebert already counted Carl Legien, the revisionist head of the General Commission of Free (Socialist) Trade Unions as a personal friend and political ally. As divisions in the party hardened between the radical left and the right, with the majority centre holding the ring, Ebert maintained an 'unpolitical' organisational stance, bureaucratic by inclination, notionally Marxist by habit, moderate by default.

The years 1910 and 1911 saw new crises for the SPD and for Germany. Attempts by the Prussian Landtag – each kingdom and principality of the Empire had its own parliament – to reform the franchise to the further detriment of the working class provoked socialist demonstrations, bringing the disagreements between moderates and radicals into sharper focus. In July 1911 Germany despatched the warship *Panther* to Agadir, ostensibly to protect its interests in Morocco, in reality to undermine French influence. The British Chancellor of the Exchequer David Lloyd George issued Germany a bellicose warning. Sceptical of Austria-Hungary's value as an ally, the Kaiser and his advisers drew back, settling for a compensatory slice of the Congo, an accelerated naval building programme and enlargement of the army.

Ebert now faced a further setback in his career. Paul Singer, the party co-chairman who had first identified Ebert's potential, died in 1911. The trade union leader Legien saw in his friend Ebert the ideal candidate to take Singer's place: sympathetic to the trade unions and the revisionists but retaining credibility with the Marxist centre. Legien nominated him at the 1911 Jena party congress, citing above all his administrative abilities. Ebert rose and declared himself unwilling, urging support for Hugo Haase, a candidate backed by the centre and left of the party. Bebel, who had blocked Ebert's path temporarily in 1904, made it clear he preferred Haase's more reliable ideological credentials. Haase won 283 of the 393 delegates' votes, but Ebert – despite declining nomination – still took 102, a marker for the future.

Ebert remained a party secretary. In the event, Haase's election as co-chairman placed greater authority in Ebert's hands. Bebel, the pillar of the left in the party leadership was now in his seventies and spent much of his time in Switzerland, returning to Germany only when the Reichstag was in session. Haase was reluctant to abandon a flourishing legal practice and devoted no more than a few hours a week to party affairs, leaving Ebert the dominant figure on the executive. Relations between Ebert and Haase were strained from the start, a foretaste of the break in the party that would erupt in a few years.

> 'What he wanted done, he got done almost always, though not without a considerable angry rolling of the eyes.'
>
> **PHILIPP SCHEIDEMANN ON FRIEDRICH EBERT**

Philipp Scheidemann, also elected to the SPD executive in 1911, shared an office with Ebert and Müller. Scheidemann, while acknowledging Ebert's organisational talent, did not share his predilection for the nuts and bolts of party administration. He recalled Ebert at an executive meeting denouncing 'with amazing earnestness' the case of a minor party official who had bought new office curtains without the leadership's sanction. Discussion then moved, an exasperated Scheidemann noted, to an analysis of the salary being paid to a printing works manager. This attachment to the pettiest detail seemed not only to Ebert's taste, but a central part of his personality. Scheidemann found Ebert quick to anger and apt to bear grudges. 'What he wanted done, he got done almost always, though not without a considerable angry rolling of the eyes.' There was another side. 'Ebert,' Scheidemann wrote, 'was splendid company among those who were out to enjoy themselves. Then he would talk for hours on business and politics, and let himself go.' [15]

Ebert concentrated his attention on elections to the Reichstag due in 1912. The SPD's longstanding policy of maintaining a distance from 'bourgeois' parties was moderating as the leadership sought a genuine parliamentary government. On the eve of the elections, the executive – without informing Bebel – secretly agreed with the middle-class liberal Progressives that SPD or Progressive candidates would withdraw in the second round in constituencies where the other stood the better chance. The possibility of the alliance between socialism and liberalism that Bismarck had feared in the 1870s was looking more possible. Ebert contested Eberfeld-Barmen and was depressed at the low turnout at his meetings. The party, bruised by the 1907 losses, was careful to avoid attacks on militarism and imperialism and reaped the reward by increasing its vote from 3,259,000 to 4,250,300, and its deputies from 43 to 110, making it the largest group in the Reichstag. Ebert was returned in Eberfeld-Barmen with a substantial majority.

PHILIPP SCHEIDEMANN (1865–1939) Originally a printer and then a journalist, Scheidemann became an SPD Reichstag deputy in 1903 and a party executive member in 1906. A supporter of the war and close colleague of Ebert's, he entered Prince Max of Baden's government as minister without portfolio in October 1918. Scheidemann – to Ebert's anger – proclaimed the German Republic on 9 November. He became Chancellor in the first Weimar government in 1919 but resigned over his refusal to accept the Treaty of Versailles, never holding ministerial office again. He went into exile in Denmark when the Nazis came to power in 1933.

In the aftermath of the 1912 victory, the SPD appeared to lose momentum, though Ebert denied this. He declared at the Württemberg regional congress in July 1913, *Our opponents already speak of the stagnation of our movement. They are simply wrong. The slower growth of the organisation can be explained by the economic depression. We must pay greater attention to this trend.*[16] But the radicals insisted the party's air of impotence derived from preferring debate in the Reichstag to waging class war. Ebert responded by attempting to censor their views, using his authority over the party press. In March 1913 the executive ordered all SPD newspapers to close their columns to criticism of the leadership or the party's Reichstag deputies.

The Jena congress in September 1913 was a watershed for the SPD and for Ebert's career. The congress confirmed a reversal of the party's historic opposition to militarism and Ebert consolidated his place at its head. Bebel had died in August, leaving a vacancy for the co-chairmanship. On 20 September the party congress elected Ebert to the post with over 90 per cent of the vote, a mark of the respect in which his abilities were held, even by those who did not share his vision of the SPD's future. Ebert and Haase divided their responsibilities as co-chairman, Haase leading the SPD fraction in the Reichstag, Ebert overseeing the party apparatus.

Of more immediate significance was the change in the party's attitude towards the armed forces. The SPD Reichstag deputies had always refused to vote funds to the army and navy on the grounds that they constituted the capitalist state's repressive arm. In 1892 the then SPD chairman Singer had ended a stirring denunciation of the German state with the words, 'As far as the military budgets are concerned we say, "Not a penny and not a man for militarism, for the prevailing militaristic system."' [17] With renewed international apprehension over the 1912–13 Balkan Wars, the Army Bill of 1913 proposed an increase of 19,000 officers and 117,000 men.

In June 1913 the SPD deputies voted against the bill, though other parties in the Reichstag ensured it passed. However, the government proposed to raise the necessary finance through income, property and inheritance taxes that would have more impact on the upper and middle classes than the working class. On that basis, 52 SPD deputies voted for the taxes that made the army increases possible, while 37 – mainly on the left – voted against.

The Jena congress debated the actions of the 52 deputies over two days in September 1913. The radicals criticised the deputies, arguing that supporting the finance bill had made a mockery of the party's anti-militarism. The moderates argued that had the SPD rejected the bill, the government would have dissolved the Reichstag, called elections and revived accusations that the party was unpatriotic. An executive resolution supporting the 52 deputies was passed by 336 votes to 140. A correspondent of *The Times* commented, 'It is at any rate pretty obvious that the German Socialist leaders have had most of the sting taken out of their anti-militarist propaganda.'[18] In an atmosphere of international tension, the SPD was demonstrating its reliability.

There was a further defeat for the radicals on the political mass strike, an issue that had plagued the executive since 1905. Ebert prepared the ground for the debate at a meeting of the party leadership before the Jena congress, arguing that while he was not in principle against the mass strike as a tactic, the time was not ripe and the party and trade unions needed a long preparatory process. Ebert's contribution to the debate at a closed session of the congress was carefully ambiguous. *In countries in which the proletariat has nothing to lose but everything to gain, the political strike is certainly the proper and effective means. It teaches the proletariat to know its own strength and its significance in the productive process. In Germany, however, the proletariat has something to lose, indeed much, even if it is only limited rights and its own organisation.*[19] Revolution, he implied, was a threat to the party rather than its mission.

There was an interesting incident after the congress, one suggesting that the government regarded Ebert as a malleable figure. The SPD Reichstag fraction had named the radical Karl Liebknecht as its spokesman on military supply budgets. A committed anti-militarist, Liebknecht had been imprisoned in 1907 for high treason for publishing a pamphlet attacking the army, and had recently exposed corruption in military contracts. The Interior Ministry asked Haase to withdraw Liebknecht, but he refused. The government then turned to Ebert, presumably calculating that he would take a different view, but he seconded what Haase had said. However, Ebert would be more obliging to the government in the coming international crisis.

2
The War, 1914–18

Historians have long debated the responsibility for the outbreak of war in 1914. The framers of the Treaty of Versailles in 1919, the victors, had no doubt that Germany should bear the burden, though they never used the words 'war guilt'. Of the European powers that went to war, perhaps only Belgium could plead innocence. Military, diplomatic and domestic considerations lead each government to conclude that war was an answer to the problems confronting them in the summer of 1914. But it was Germany's leaders who had been pursuing a policy in which conflict with France and Russia was seen as an inevitable necessity.

The immediate trigger for the international crisis of 1914 was the assassination of Archduke Franz Ferdinand, heir apparent to the throne of Austria-Hungary, in Sarajevo on 28 June. The conspirators had been armed by Serbian military intelligence. Most European governments acknowledged Austria-Hungary's right to act firmly against Serbia in the wake of the murder. On 6 July the German Chancellor Theobald von Bethmann-Hollweg assured Austria-Hungary of Germany's backing, giving what was subsequently described as a 'blank cheque'. Austria-Hungary presented Serbia with a humiliating ultimatum on 23 July, prompting Serbia to mobilise its army and seek Russian assistance. When Austria-Hungary mobilised against Serbia on 25 July, Russia – believing Germany was manipulating events to provoke a wider conflict – proceeded to muster her armies. Both Germany and her ally rejected a British proposal for a conference to resolve the dispute between Austria and Serbia.

The network of European alliances constructed before 1914 now locked in. On 1 August Germany, which had been vainly hoping to confine hostilities to the Balkans, declared war on Russia, afraid her mobilisation posed a threat. The Schlieffen Plan, drawn up by the German Chief of the General Staff in 1905, had been based on the premise of a war on two fronts against Russia and France, allies since the 1890s. The plan, though modified, now dominated. On 2 August Germany demanded passage for her troops across Belgium to confront France. The following day Germany declared war on France and entered Belgium. Britain, which had guaranteed Belgian neutrality under the 1839 Treaty of London, demanded Germany's withdrawal. Germany refused. By midnight on 4 August Austria-Hungary, Serbia, Germany, Russia, France, Britain and Belgium were engaged in the first major European conflict since 1815.

There had rarely been any question among most German

GERMANY'S RESPONSIBILITY FOR THE WAR
'From the moment the First World War began, the belligerents began publishing their own accounts of how the conflict had been caused ... Their focus was on the events of July 1914 itself, but their central debate concerned the issue of whether or not Germany was guilty of causing the war. The paradox was this: Austria-Hungary, not Germany, was the power that planned to use war as an instrument of policy ... For this Germany was blamed, both then and since.'[1]

Hew Strachan, *The First World War*

socialists that they would fight for their country if Russia were the enemy. Bebel had told the Erfurt congress in 1891, 'if Russia, the citadel of cruelty and barbarism, the foe of all human civilisation, should attack Germany in order to weaken and dismember her – and such a war could have no other aim – we should have as much or more at stake than those who are at the head of Germany, and we would resist the aggressor.' [2] But the SPD had never been forced to face the tension between internationalism and patriotism – Marx had once written that the workers had no country. When the party executive met on 29 June, the day after the Archduke's assassination, Haase alone feared events could trigger a European war. Ebert, his co-chairman, vehemently disagreed and left Berlin almost at once for a planned vacation on the Baltic island of Rügen with his wife, daughter Amalie and son Karl. Ebert's fellow executive member Scheidemann was equally sanguine, taking the train to Austria for a climbing holiday.

Only when Austria mobilised on 25 July did the SPD leadership begin to grasp the peril facing Europe. The party daily *Vorwärts* thundered, 'Not a drop of blood from a German soldier should be sacrificed to the power madness of the Austrian rulers, to imperialistic profit interests.' [3] The SPD mounted demonstrations across Germany, urging the government to restrain Austria. Bethmann-Hollweg, understanding the urgency of keeping the SPD on side, emphasised that Russia would be to blame if war broke out. As the crisis developed, the SPD executive sent a telegram to Ebert calling him back to Berlin. Fearing that the party would be outlawed in the event of war, the executive then despatched Ebert to Zurich on 30 July to prepare to keep the SPD alive in exile. His friend Müller, meanwhile, travelled to Paris to ascertain the attitude of the French socialists. The French said their position depended on whether their country was attacked. The SPD and the trade unions were adopting a similar stance. On 31 July, as the Imperial government imposed martial law, an SPD regional newspaper warned, 'We do not want our wives and children to be sacrificed to the bestialities of the Cossacks.'[4]

The SPD leadership now faced a crucial decision. On 31 July and 2 August the party executive and Reichstag deputies discussed their response to the government's request for 5,000 million marks in war credits. Haase, Ebert's co-chairman, advised voting against. Although this would have no impact, as the majority of the Reichstag would support the government, it would affect the government's attitude towards the SPD. They might even be international repercussions, with socialists overseas deciding to follow the leading Marxist party. Ebert, still in Switzerland, was not involved in the anguished debate. On 3 August 78 of the 92 SPD Reichstag members agreed to support the government's request for credits. Haase, the party's leader in the Reichstag, was among the 14 opponents.

> **In defending our country we protect the vital interests of the German worker.**
>
> **EBERT, AUGUST 1914**

It nevertheless fell to Haase to declare the SPD's support for the war in the Reichstag on 4 August. He blamed the arms race for the antagonisms that had led to international conflict, but acknowledged the threat Russian despotism posed. 'Our task is to ward off this danger, to safeguard the civilisation and the independence of our own country. And here we make good what we have always emphatically affirmed: we do not leave the Fatherland in the lurch in the hour of danger.'[5] Bethmann-Hollweg revealed later in the debate that German armies were already marching into Belgium. The SPD deputies, whose support had been based on what they believed to be a defensive struggle, made no comment. Ebert, now back in Berlin, declared, *In defending our country we protect the vital interests of the German worker.* He agreed war would cause distress to the working class, but said this would be temporary and paled into insignificance beside the miseries defeat would bring.[6]

By casting their vote for war, Ebert's party had made a decision that would not only govern its role in the conflict but set the scene for its actions in the November 1918 revolution and define post-war Germany. Established as the enemy of the capitalist state, the SPD now welcomed the embrace of that state in the name of self-defence. As the war progressed that embrace would tighten until the SPD leadership, Ebert above all, proved unable to think outside the state's impera-tives. Reading the news of the German's party's acquiescence in August 1914, the Bolshevik leader Lenin thought the paper was a forgery. For Europe's leading Marxist party to abandon the principle of internationalism condemned the 25-year-old Socialist International to death.

The rewards of what became known as the *Burgfrieden*, the 'peace of the castle', were immediate, if limited. The gov-ernment lifted the ban on SPD literature in army barracks and promised, vaguely, reform of the Prussian electoral system. Trade union leaders abandoned strikes for the duration and were welcomed into the state's administrative machinery to police their members in the war industries. Ebert, virtually unknown outside the party before 1914, entered the ante-chamber of power, consulted and flattered by Imperial politi-cians, high bureaucrats and senior army officers.

Five months after the outbreak of war Ebert explained the origins of the catastrophe to his constituents. It was a model of current Marxist orthodoxy: accurate in a mechanical, fatalistic way, allowing Ebert to evade any specific German responsibility. *All great capitalistic states have registered an increased expansion in their economic life during the last decade. Industry and trade have pushed more than ever across their own national boundaries. The fight for markets was fought more intensively. In conjunction with the fight for markets ran the fight for territory. The division of parts of Africa and East Asia became more and more the burning issues of world politics. So the economic conflicts led to political conflicts, to continued gigantic armament increases and finally to world war.*[7] Ebert's account begged the question why, if the roots of war lay in capitalism and imperialism, the anti-capitalist and anti-imperialist SPD had plunged so wholeheartedly into the *mêlée*. The answer was patriotism, loyalty – as radicals argued – to one set of capitalist masters over another.

Rosa Luxemburg – incarcerated until 1918 for her anti-war activities – wrote scathingly that the SPD leaders had recast Marx and Engels' *Communist Manifesto* to read, 'Proletarians of all countries unite in peacetime and cut each other's throats in war'.[8] Ebert threw himself at once into efforts to persuade socialists in neutral countries – the Netherlands, Sweden, Switzerland and, for the moment, Italy – of the justice of the German cause. He did not consider the SPD had abandoned any fundamental beliefs. *In our dealings with the regime we only have guarded our rights and not made any deals ... At any rate, we have preserved the honour of the party. If peace comes again, or if the party should be faced with a catastrophe, we will take up the battle with an untarnished shield.*[9] One German socialist observed after being awarded the Iron Cross, 'How will anyone be able to say we do not love our fatherland when after the war so and so many thousands of our good party comrades say, "We have been decorated for bravery."' [10]

∞∞∞

By late 1914 Germany had successfully held Russia back, but the advance into France had stalled. The contending armies faced each other in a struggle of attrition in trenches stretching from Switzerland to the English Channel. Ebert could claim to have defended domestic working class interests, with the SPD acting as a pressure group to maintain the morale essential if the country were to wage a protracted struggle. In January 1915 Ebert, Scheidemann and the trade union leader Legien persuaded the Imperial interior secretary that the *Burgfrieden* could not be maintained without state control of wheat production, price controls and bread rationing. By June rationing was in force. The SPD similarly took up complaints about food for the fighting men. In September 1915 Ebert and three party leaders secured permission to talk to soldiers in northern France without their officers present. Ebert was satisfied that the mission secured

> We remain loyal to the Fatherland until the enemy is ready to make peace.
> **EBERT, JANUARY 1915**

improvements. But a photographer captured the embarrassing scene of Ebert and his colleagues dining at an officers' club in Zeebrugge. Radicals in Berlin reproduced the picture alongside that of an imprisoned anti-war activist, contrasting their treatment by the authorities.

The SPD leadership proclaimed, as it would throughout the war, that it favoured a 'peace of understanding'. When France declared the return of Alsace-Lorraine – seized by Prussia in 1871 – a war aim, Ebert complained in January 1915, *The*

*French Social Democratic Party are today in full sail on the
tide of Chauvinism ... We remain loyal to the Fatherland till
the enemy is ready to make peace.*[11] There were increasingly
strident demands from the Pan-German right to hold on to the
conquests her armies had made, extending post-war German
rule to the Baltic provinces, Belgium and northern France, the
Balkans and the Ukraine. Bethmann-Hollweg remained silent
on the issue, unwilling to alienate the SPD.

In May 1915 Italy, formerly a member of the Triple Alliance with Germany and Austria-Hungary but hitherto
neutral, joined the Allies, persuaded by the secret offer of
substantial territorial gains. In a debate on a request for
further war credits on 28 May Ebert reiterated SPD support
for the government but repeated the socialist desire for peace
and no territorial annexations by either side. The following
month Haase – Ebert's co-chairman – and the party's leading
Marxist theoretician, Kautsky, published a manifesto criticising the SPD's policy. At a subsequent executive meeting Ebert
harangued Haase brutally. Kautsky complained that Ebert
was using the war and his close relation with the government
to purge the SPD of Marxism in the guise of disciplining anti-
war radicals.

The government's persistent need for war credits heightened the rift tearing the SPD apart. On 22 December 20 of the
party's Reichstag deputies rejected the government's demand
and 22 abstained, Ebert leading the remainder in support.
The party executive justified its continuing backing for the
war: 'Our enemies show no disposition to peace; on the con-
trary, they persist in their intention to ruin Germany and its
allies in an economic and military sense.' The trade unions,
their influence in the party growing stronger, said Germany
still faced the peril of invasion and 'the doom involved in an

unhappy end to the war, which would burden us for decades to come with war indemnities'.[12]

Anxious to break the stalemate on the Western Front, Germany launched an offensive against the French at Verdun in February 1916. The battle raged on inconclusively into the summer, with massive losses on both sides. In July Britain and France opened an attack on the Somme with, again, heavy casualties and little to show for it. With progress on the Western Front checked and the German population suffering from a British naval blockade, the military authorities proposed an expansion of the U-boat campaign, claiming that submarines could sink 600,000 tons of shipping a month and bring Britain to her knees. Ebert endorsed the proposal, telling the Reichstag, *Here we are fighting for our existence. We have right on our side if we reply to the British hunger blockade with the U-boat war. No one can complain about that ... Britain is making ruthless use of the right of capture at sea. The U-boat war is only a measure of self-defence against that.*[13] The government held back for the moment, fearing the reaction of the United States, but ordered unrestricted U-boat attacks in January 1917.

The SPD was now at breaking-point. On 24 March 1916 a substantial minority of the party's Reichstag deputies rejected the government's request for war credits. The SPD fraction voted 58 to 33 to exclude the rebels. The following day Ebert replaced Haase as SPD leader in the Reichstag. He appealed for unity, saying the party had done all in its power to end the war but Germany's enemies showed no desire for peace. As bitterness between the socialist factions heightened, and war-weariness set in, the authorities intensified arrests of radicals, among them Liebknecht after he led the first public anti-war demonstration in May 1916. One historian notes, 'majority

Socialists completely ignored the arrests ... In a few cases they even pointed out dangerous opponents to the police.' [14]

At a party conference in Berlin in September Ebert denounced radicals organising strikes in munitions factories. He said the party leadership had consistently opposed a war of conquest and had worked to persuade Allied socialists to press their governments to end the conflict. Ebert painted a grim picture of a defeated Germany. *Our land would suffer terribly, its economic progress would be arrested and crushing taxation laid upon us. What would then happen to Socialism? What good would a just redistribution of wealth do for us in a land whose people would have to deliver the greater part of its goods, not to capitalists at home, but to conquerors abroad?* [15] In October the party in the Reichstag voted once more for war credits, but Ebert associated the SPD's support with a demand for price controls and more efficient food distribution.

> **What good would a just redistribution of wealth do for us in a land whose people would have to deliver the greater part of its goods, not to capitalists at home, but to conquerors abroad?**
>
> **EBERT, SEPTEMBER 1916**

ooooo

By late 1916 the Chief of the General Staff, Field Marshal Paul von Hindenburg, and his deputy, General Erich Ludendorff, were at the head of an unofficial military dictatorship. One historian has described this 'silent dictatorship' as standing 'halfway between the bonapartism of Bismarck and the fascist dictatorship of Hitler'. [16] The increasing involvement of military commanders in organising munitions production drew them into co-ordinating the overall economy. The

Auxiliary Service Act – masterminded by General Wilhelm Groener (a rising star at the Prussian Ministry of War) and partly drafted by the trade union leader Carl Legien, a close friend of Ebert's for many years – introduced conscription of male workers into the war industries and expanded the use of prisoners of war and enforced labour from occupied Belgium and Poland. The trade unions received greater recognition by the state in return for their co-operation. Party leaders heartily favoured the Act, the SPD daily *Vorwärts* declaring that it was a milestone on the road to state socialism.

Ebert developed relations with Groener that were to have significant repercussions for Germany. As *Vorwärts* had inferred, a hybrid politico-military 'Prussian socialism' was emerging. 'It would not be impossible,' one historian suggests, 'for the officer corps to come to terms with the Social Democratic Party under such a system, a party whose exceptional discipline and organisation owed much to the son of a non-commissioned officer, August Bebel, and which was not as far removed from the Prussian military tradition as its leaders wished to think.' [17] When Groener was dismissed in August 1917, SPD deputies in the Reichstag complained

WILHELM GROENER (1867–1939)
The son of a non-commissioned officer, Groener joined the army in 1884. In 1914 he was responsible for the railway movement of troops on the Western and Eastern Fronts. In May 1916 he became head of food supplies in Germany and subsequently took charge of the Supreme War Bureau, co-ordinating industry and labour under the Hindenburg-Ludendorff 'silent dictatorship'. After army commands in France and the Ukraine, Groener became Hindenburg's deputy in October 1918, advising the Kaiser to abdicate in November and acting as a crucial link between the army and Ebert. Entering politics after his resignation from the army, Groener held the posts of transport minister from 1920–3, defence minister in 1928 and interior minister in 1931. He was forced out of office in 1932 after an attempt to ban the Nazi Brownshirts.

he had been removed because of his sympathy towards labour and his efforts to curb excessive profits in the war industries.

The Allies having rejected a tentative but unacceptable German peace proposal in December 1916, Ebert told a Reichstag debate on war aims in February 1917 that the Entente powers would be satisfied only with Germany's complete subjection. *In view of this state of affairs, German Social Democracy again declares its determination to hold out until a peace that will safeguard the vital interests of the German people is achieved.*[18] The overthrow of the Tsar in Russia in March 1917 raised hopes that peace, and even democratic reform in Germany, might be closer than the SPD had believed. But it also raised questions about the party's justification of their support for the war – self-defence against the Tsarist autocracy. Ebert hesitated and then agreed to send a congratulatory telegram to the Russian revolutionary government on 21 March. A week later, four parties in the Reichstag – the SPD, the Catholic Centre, the National Liberals and the Progressives – established a 28-strong committee to press for constitutional reform. Events were now moving fast. On 6 April the SPD's minority dissidents – led by Haase, Kautsky and Bernstein – formally split from the majority, establishing the Independent Social Democratic Party (USPD). Ebert succeeded Haase as the SPD's senior co-chairman; Scheidemann was elected to the second chairmanship.

Ebert and Scheidemann were, meanwhile, putting out feelers in neutral Denmark to determine whether the new Russian government was prepared to make peace with Germany. There can be no doubt that the SPD were working for their own government in their mission – the Foreign Office provided passes for the journey to Copenhagen and the Foreign

Minister told the deputation how delighted he was with their plan. The United States' declaration of war on Germany on 6 April – provoked by the impact of unrestricted U-boat war and anger at German meddling in Central America – added a new urgency to pacifying the Eastern Front. Ebert became acquainted in Copenhagen with the German ambassador to Denmark, Count Ulrich von Brockdorff-Rantzau, a diplomat who sympathised with the desire for parliamentary democracy. He had opposed the gamble Germany had taken in resorting to unrestricted submarine warfare, fearing its effect on the attitude of neutral governments. Ebert's mission failed as Russia's new rulers continued the war. However, during his stay a party of Russian exiles passed through Copenhagen *en route* to Petrograd from Switzerland under German government auspices. The group included the Bolshevik leader Lenin, whom Ebert declined to meet, pleading pressing business in Berlin.

The pressing business was a strike being prepared in the war industries. Following the failure of the 1916 harvest, the population suffered the 'turnip winter', with turnips (until now seen as food fit only for animals) replacing potatoes. Rations fell in February 1917 to 1,000 calories per person daily. On 14 April Ebert and Scheidemann told a minister that the strike, organised by radical shop stewards in defiance of trade union leaders, was unavoidable. A further reduction in the bread ration had been the last straw for workers who had been radicalised by events in Russia and had no confidence in the Kaiser's renewed promises of political reform. On 16 April 125,000 workers struck in Berlin, 18,000 in Leipzig, and thousands more in other industrial centres. The government deployed troops in the factories to crush the strike movement. In the wake of the unrest, more party branches seceded to join the minority Independents, strengthening the position of the right in the majority SPD.

In June Scandinavian and Dutch socialists (prompted by the SPD, with the German government in the shadows) mounted a conference in Stockholm to discuss ways of ending the war. Britain and France refused to allow their socialists to attend but Ebert led the SPD delegation, which included Scheidemann, Müller and Legien. At the first meeting on 4 June Ebert refused to consider the question of responsibility for the war, saying the business in hand was peace, not apportioning blame. The SPD said in a memorandum presented on 12 June that the party sought a peace with no annexations and no indemnities. Alsace-Lorraine was to remain German, as were the German districts of Poland. Germany's overseas colonies – now occupied by Allied forces – were to be returned, but Ireland, Egypt and India were to be given independence by Britain, along with Morocco by France, and Poland and Finland by Russia. Germany would not pay for war damage inflicted in Belgium and France, but would be prepared to contribute to an international relief fund. Ebert and the SPD delegation left Stockholm the following day, having made it plain that the peace they sought would leave the German Empire unhindered. Ebert and his colleagues were, however, impressed by the certainty of neutral Socialists that Germany would lose the war. A month later the Kaiser congratulated Ebert and Scheidemann over cigars, 'You did fine work; you've had a fine passage of arms.'[19]

We are at the end of our strength; peace must be reached as soon as possible.

EBERT, JULY 1917

The political crisis reached a high point in July with a 'peace resolution', the fruit of growing collaboration between the SPD and liberal middle class parties in the Reichstag. On 3 July Ebert said the April strikes had demonstrated the extent of distress and disillusion, warning, *Malnutrition has reached dangerous levels, the health of the workers has been badly shattered ... We are at the end of our strength; peace must be reached as soon as possible.*[20] Matthias Erzberger, leader of the Catholic Centre Party, told the Reichstag on 6 July that the U-boat war had failed to achieve victory and that everything should be done to negotiate peace by the end of 1917. Chancellor Bethmann-Hollweg – harried by the military command – resigned, succeeded by the army's nominee Georg Michaelis. On 19 July the three major parties – the SPD, the Centre and the Progressives – carried a resolution by 214 to 116 declaring, 'The Reichstag strives for a peace of understanding and the permanent reconciliation of the peoples. With such a peace forced acquisitions of territory and political, economic, or financial oppressions are inconsistent.'[21] The following day the parties voted the government further war credits.

The Kaiser quickly revealed the lack of significance he – and Germany's effective rulers, Hindenburg and Ludendorff – attached to the 'peace resolution'. On 20 July he held a reception for Reichstag party leaders, including Ebert. Full of bonhomie, the Kaiser said Russia could not make revolution and fight simultaneously. Ebert, though flattered by the attention, was alarmed at the Kaiser's bombast, reporting to Scheidemann, *When HE has defeated all the others, HE will start a second Punic War and finish off England.*[22] A mutiny in August by sailors in the High Seas Fleet at Wilhelmshaven was ruthlessly suppressed. Ebert bitterly condemned the government in a debate in October after Michaelis threatened to outlaw the Independent Socialists for allegedly fomenting the mutiny. *I say openly, we shall welcome each day that will bring us closer to freeing the German people from this government.*[23] Count Georg von Hertling replaced Michaelis as Chancellor in November.

ooooo

As Michaelis was leaving office, Lenin's Bolsheviks seized power in a coup in Petrograd, guaranteeing – as the German authorities had confidently expected – Russia's exit from the war. While radicals welcomed what they believed to be a socialist revolution, the military looked eagerly to the Ukraine, Finland and the Baltic states falling into Germany's hands. A further significant event came on 8 January 1918 when United States' President Woodrow Wilson, aware of the possible impact of events in Russia, put his peace proposals to a joint session of Congress – the Fourteen Points.

The German government rejected Wilson's proposals out of hand. The Chancellor, Hertling, saw little need to even consider a negotiated peace. 'Our brilliant military leaders view the future with undiminished confidence in victory.'[24] The Catholic Centre Party accused Wilson of bullying. *Vorwärts*, the SPD daily, reacted less aggressively but the party as a whole was divided in its reaction. No sooner had Wilson announced his proposals than Germany faced a fresh wave of strikes, the exhausted workers influenced by Wilson's proposals, events in Russia and a cut in the bread ration. The first strike began in Berlin on 28 January, as 400,000 workers downed tools. Later that day, strikers' representatives demanded an immediate peace without annexations or reparations. The strike spread rapidly to Munich, Kiel, Hamburg and other industrial centres. Ebert opposed the strike but accepted an invitation to join the strike committee in Berlin, hoping to limit its extent, keep authority out of radical hands, and bring the action to a speedy end. By 4 February the strike had been broken by the military, with many leading participants – though not Ebert – imprisoned or conscripted.

Ebert revealed his personal feelings about the strike in a letter to his son Georg at the front. *Our troops have earned the everlasting gratitude of the nation. During the last few days some senseless strikes have broken out here in consequence of the reduction of the bread ration. Such fools' strikes do not serve the cause of peace, but only strengthen the fighting spirit of the enemy.*[25] The letter was returned to Ebert unopened. His son had been killed in action.

The Treaty of Brest-Litovsk – signed by Russia with Germany and her allies Austria-Hungary, Turkey and Bulgaria on 3 March 1918 – revealed the harsh terms that could be expected of a victorious Germany. Russia lost a third of her population – surrendering the Ukraine, the Baltic provinces, Finland, Poland and the Caucasus – half her manufacturing, the bulk of her coalfields and fertile agricultural areas in the west. Russia was subsequently ordered to pay Germany six billion marks in reparations for war damage. Ebert would say privately, *The Brest Treaty is and remains a misfortune,*[26] but he was prepared to support the settlement, using the contrived argument that to vote against it would be to oppose peace. The SPD avoided a further split by abstaining; the breakaway Independents voted against. On 7 May Germany imposed the Treaty of Bucharest on Romania, seizing much of the country's territory and imposing a heavy indemnity. Led by Ebert, the SPD supported ratification of the treaty in the Reichstag.

Germany opened a major offensive on the Western Front on 21 March, hoping to make gains before significant numbers of

PRESIDENT WILSON'S FOURTEEN POINTS, 8 JANUARY 1918

The program of the world's peace, therefore, is our program; and that program, the only possible program, as we see it, is this:

I. Open covenants of peace, openly arrived at, after which there shall be no private international understandings of any kind but diplomacy shall proceed always frankly and in the public view.

II. Absolute freedom of navigation upon the seas, outside territorial waters, alike in peace and in war, except as the seas may be closed in whole or in part by international action for the enforcement of international covenants.

III. The removal, so far as possible, of all economic barriers and the establishment of an equality of trade conditions among all the nations consenting to the peace and associating themselves for its maintenance.

IV. Adequate guarantees given and taken that national armaments will be reduced to the lowest point consistent with domestic safety.

V. A free, open-minded, and absolutely impartial adjustment of all colonial claims, based upon a strict observance of the principle that in determining all such questions of sovereignty the interests of the populations concerned must have equal weight with the equitable claims of the government whose title is to be determined.

VI. The evacuation of all Russian territory and such a settlement of all questions affecting Russia as will secure the best and freest cooperation of the other nations of the world in obtaining for her an unhampered and unembarrassed opportunity for the independent determination of her own political development and national policy and assure her of a sincere welcome into the society of free nations under institutions of her own choosing; and, more than a welcome, assistance also of every kind that she may need and may herself desire. The treatment accorded Russia by her sister nations in the months to come will be the acid test of their good will, of their comprehension of her needs as distinguished from their own interests, and of their intelligent and unselfish sympathy.

VII. Belgium, the whole world will agree, must be evacuated and restored, without any attempt to limit the sovereignty which she enjoys in common with all other free nations. No other single act will serve as this will serve to restore confidence among the nations in the laws which they have themselves set and determined for the government of their relations with one another. Without this healing act the whole structure and validity of international law is forever impaired.

VIII. All French territory should be freed and the invaded portions restored, and the wrong done to France by Prussia in 1871 in the matter of Alsace-Lorraine, which has unsettled the peace of the world for nearly fifty years, should be righted, in order that peace may once more be made secure in the interest of all.

IX. A readjustment of the frontiers of Italy should be effected along clearly recognizable lines of nationality.

X. The peoples of Austria-Hungary, whose place among the nations we wish to see safeguarded and assured, should be accorded the freest opportunity to autonomous development.

XI. Rumania, Serbia, and Montenegro should be evacuated; occupied territories restored; Serbia accorded free and secure access to the sea; and the relations of the several Balkan states to one another determined by friendly counsel along historically established lines of allegiance and nationality; and international guarantees of the political and economic independence and territorial integrity of the several Balkan states should be entered into.

XII. The Turkish portion of the present Ottoman Empire should be assured a secure sovereignty, but the other nationalities which are now under Turkish rule should be assured an undoubted security of life and an absolutely unmolested opportunity of autonomous development, and the Dardanelles should be permanently opened as a free passage to the ships and commerce of all nations under international guarantees.

XIII. An independent Polish state should be erected which should include the territories inhabited by indisputably Polish populations, which should be assured a free and secure access to the sea, and whose political and economic independence and territorial integrity should be guaranteed by international covenant.

XIV. A general association of nations must be formed under specific covenants for the purpose of affording mutual guarantees of political independence and territorial integrity to great and small states alike.

American troops arrived in France. In March and July Ebert led the SPD in voting for further war credits, blaming the Allied governments on 13 July for continuing the fight. *They are misleading their peoples as regards Germany's power of resistance. Since our enemies refuse a peace that would be honourable for all, we shall again sanction the means for the achievement of peace.*[27]

Over the summer of 1918 the tide turned against Germany as Allied counterattacks bludgeoned her armies. On 13 August Hindenburg, Ludendorff and Hertling agreed Germany had no choice but to open peace negotiations with the Allies. It was necessary now to conjure up the appearance of democratic government to ensure favourable terms. On 23 September the SPD discussed participation in a new administration, though certainly not one led by Hertling. Uppermost in Ebert's mind was the fear that collapse in Germany would lead to the revolutionary chaos taking place in Russia. *We must throw ourselves into the breach and see whether we will receive enough influence to push through our demands.*[28] Rumours in Berlin that Hertling was to be replaced by Count Brockdorff-Rantzau, with Ebert as interior minister, came to nothing. Hertling resigned on 29 September. He was replaced by the relatively unknown but liberal Prince Max of Baden, the Kaiser's cousin, who attempted to pull together an administration made up of the parties that had co-operated in the July 1917 'peace resolution'.

On 2 October, as the SPD hesitated over joining Prince Max, a senior officer revealed the extent of the army's defeat in the field to a meeting of Reichstag party leaders. He said an armistice had to be concluded before the Allies realised Germany's military weakness. Ebert, hardly believing what he had heard, hurried to the SPD executive committee, white-faced and tearful. Despite Scheidemann's warning against joining a 'bankrupt concern', the committee agreed to enter Prince Max's government, unanimously shouting 'Ebert' when a delegate called for the party's best man to be drafted. Ebert nominated Scheidemann and Otto Bauer. Prince Max contacted President Wilson via the Swiss government on 3 October, seeking an armistice as a preliminary to negotiations based on the Fourteen Points – which the German government had rejected in January – and nine principles he had subsequently added. Ebert doubted the American's sincerity, telling Prince Max, *Wilson disguises his policies cleverly, but he is still an imperialist.*[29] Exchanges of notes through October and early November showed Wilson would only parley with a democratic Germany and implied that the Kaiser's abdication was a precondition of peace.

> **We want the coming peace to be a firm and eternal compact of free and equal people.**
>
> **EBERT, OCTOBER 1918**

In a speech to the final session of the Imperial Reichstag on 22 October Ebert said that without peace there would be revolution, but he warned the Allies not to push Germany too hard. *If (the other people of Europe) want to remain our enemies, treat us as the scum of humanity, and take us as their peons, we tell them: watch out, every servitude comes to an end … We want the coming peace to be a firm and eternal compact of free and equal people … If we are disappointed in this goal, we will not give up, because we believe in our people and we will stand with them in loyalty, until liberty comes.*[30] Ludendorff, who had first pressed Prince Max to seek an armistice, now changed his mind and resigned on 26 October. His successor was Groener, whom the SPD leaders respected and believed they could trust. Groener, in turn, was

Revolution in Berlin: midday 9 November 1918

confident he could rely on the SPD to safeguard the essential elements of a decaying system, above all the interests of the officer class.

3

Defeat and Revolution, 1918–19

Germany had now achieved what Ebert saw as the SPD's major objective, a constitutional monarchy with a government answerable to the Reichstag. On 5 October the population – weary, malnourished, prey to the influenza epidemic beginning to sweep Europe – were finally told their government was seeking an armistice. But on 29 October German naval commanders ordered the fleet out of harbour for a final 'death or glory' challenge to the Anglo-American fleet in the North Sea. Two ships' crews mutinied at sea, were overpowered and returned to Kiel for court martial. Shipyard workers and sailors at the port demonstrated in the streets demanding their release and on 4 November a council of sailors and workers took control of the town. The government sent Gustav Noske, the right-wing SPD deputy, to Kiel to prevent rebellion becoming revolution. Noske persuaded the sailors' and workers' council to appoint him military governor.

Ebert and the SPD leaders renewed their friendly relations with Groener following a cabinet meeting on 6 November. Ebert told Groener that only the Kaiser's abdication could prevent revolution; the SPD would accept a parliamentary monarchy with a regent on the throne. As they were talking, Scheidemann interrupted with a report that the Kiel revolt was spreading and councils of workers, soldiers and sailors now controlled Cuxhaven, Wilhelmshaven, Hamburg and Hanover. All made the same demands: peace, democracy and an end to the monarchy. Ebert urged Groener to reconsider his opposition to the Kaiser abdicating but the general remained adamant. A disappointed Ebert said, *Under the circumstances any further discussion is superfluous … We will always remember with pleasure our work with you during the war.*[1] Ebert discussed the situation with Prince Max the following afternoon in the Chancellery garden. The Chancellor said he intended to persuade the Kaiser to give up the throne and asked Ebert if he could count on him to prevent revolution. Ebert replied, *Unless the Kaiser abdicates, the social revolution is inevitable. But I will have none of it; I hate it like sin.*[2] In Bavaria the king had already fled, leaving the Independent Kurt Eisner at the head of a revolutionary government.

Ebert was already contemplating the danger to the SPD of taking sole responsibility for a peace that was likely to be unpopular. He told the party's Reichstag faction on 7 November that he proposed no action until an armistice had been reached. But on 8 November representatives of the Revolutionary Shop Stewards, the organisers of the January 1918 strike, told Ebert they would be leading the Berlin workers in street demonstrations the following day. A delegation of soldiers urged the SPD to take power to prevent a Bolshevik-style coup. At 9 a.m. on 9 November the SPD formed a 12-strong

> **Unless the Kaiser abdicates, the social revolution is inevitable. But I will have none of it; I hate it like sin.**
>
> **EBERT, 7 NOVEMBER 1918**

council to manage what now appeared an inevitable revolution. The party's representatives in Prince Max's government resigned. At a meeting with the Chancellor, Ebert demanded that he stand down in favour of a Socialist. The Prince suggested Ebert himself. 'Herr Ebert, I am entrusting you with the German Empire.' Ebert responded, *I have lost two sons for this Empire*.[3] As armed soldiers and striking workers occupied the centre of Berlin, Prince Max told a journalist at noon that the Kaiser had agreed to abdicate (though this was, as yet, untrue), that Ebert would take office as Imperial Chancellor and preparations would be made for early elections to a constituent assembly.

It was Groener who secured the Kaiser's abdication late on 9 November at supreme military headquarters in Belgium. He and Hindenburg had now concluded that abdication was essential but sat in silence as the Kaiser fantasised about deploying troops to quell the rebels in Berlin. Groener said this was impossible, convincing Wilhelm that he had lost the army rank-and-file's loyalty. Wilhelm reluctantly signed the abdication document that evening and prepared for exile in the Netherlands. Within days all Germany's crowns had tumbled: the King of Bavaria had gone on 8 November, followed by the Kaiser, the Duke of Brunswick, the King of Württemberg, the King of Saxony, the Grand Duke of Oldenburg, the Grand Duke of Mecklenburg-Schwerin, the Prince of Reuss, the Grand Duke of Saxe-Weimar and Eisenach, the Prince of Lippe-Detmol, the Prince of Waldeck-Pyrmont, the Duke of Anhalt and, finally, the Grand Duke of Baden.

Scheidemann, meanwhile, shattered Ebert's hopes that Germany would remain a monarchy. Ebert and Scheidemann left the meeting with Prince Max on 9 November for lunch in the Reichstag dining hall. A group of workers and soldiers

Philipp Scheidemann proclaims the German Republic from the balcony of the Reichstag in Berlin, 9 November 1918

took Scheidemann aside, warning him that Liebknecht, now released from prison and leading the radical Spartacist League, was about to proclaim a Soviet Republic from the royal palace balcony. Scheidemann, saying nothing to Ebert, went to an open window and addressed the crowd below. 'The old and the rotten – the monarchy – has broken down. Long live the new! Long live the German Republic.' Scheidemann described Ebert's angry reaction. 'Ebert's face turned livid with wrath when he heard what I had done. He banged his fist on the table and yelled at me, *Is it true?*' Scheidemann replied that it was an inevitable step. *You have no right to proclaim the Republic. What becomes of Germany – whether she becomes a Republic or something else – a Constituent Assembly must decide.*[4] Ebert was not being entirely honest and knew in his own mind what he preferred. Before becoming Imperial Chancellor he had said, *The German people is not yet ready for a republic and first must be educated up to that level. That could best happen under a democratic monarchy.*[5]

ooooo

Having been handed office at the age of 47, Ebert now had to secure power. A misconception underlying his and much of the SPD's Marxism was that the organs of the capitalist state – the higher bureaucracy, the army command, the judiciary – were neutral instruments. The party would win a Reichstag majority, take political command of the state machinery, and proceed to construct socialism. Even in the best of circumstances that had been unlikely; Ebert was acting in the worst of circumstances. He appealed to the bureaucracy to support him:

The new government has taken charge of the administration to preserve the German people from civil war and famine and to accomplish their legitimate claim to autonomy. The government can solve this problem only if all the officials in town and country will help. I know it will be difficult for some to work with the new men who have taken charge of the empire, but I appeal to their love of the people ... I demand everyone's support in the hard task awaiting us.[6] Ebert would maintain his reliance on the bureaucracy of the old state, ignoring demands from SPD members, Independents and the councils to at least purge the most notorious anti-democratic personalities. Ebert saw food as central to the government's survival and as a guarantee of order. With little more than three weeks' supply in the country's reserves, he judged that only experienced public officials had the organisational skills to maintain supplies and transport.

The second element of the state that Ebert felt he had to rely on was the military command, a task eased by wartime co-operation with Groener, now army chief of staff. Ebert sat alone in his private office in the Chancellery on the evening of 9 November. A telephone, connected directly to supreme military headquarters at Spa, rang. It was Groener. He told Ebert that Hindenburg had assumed command of the army from the Kaiser and proposed to return the troops in good order to Germany once the armistice had been signed. Groener implied, in so many words, that Hindenburg and therefore the army recognised the republic. Ebert asked what was required of the government. Groener replied that Hindenburg expected it to support his officers in maintaining military discipline, adding, 'The officer corps expects that the imperial government will fight against Bolshevism and places itself at the disposal of the government for such a purpose.' Ebert asked Groener to convey his thanks to Hindenburg.[7]

On 10 November the Independents agreed to join Ebert's six-strong provisional administration, nominally answerable to the Berlin executive committee of the soldiers' and workers' councils. A councils' conference agreed that the government – the Council of People's Commissars – would comprise Ebert, Scheidemann and Otto Landsberg of the SPD and Haase, Wilhelm Dittmann and Emil Barth of the Independents. Ebert abandoned the title Imperial Chancellor for that of Chairman of the Council of People's Commissars and took specific responsibility for internal and military affairs. On 11 November the SPD paper *Vorwärts* reported Ebert's assertion *Germany has completed her revolution*. One writer describes the confident satisfaction of the country's new leader in his

Germany has completed her revolution.

EBERT, 11 NOVEMBER 1918

frock coat, 'soberly posed, a slope-shouldered parliamentarian, his coat sitting heavy and dark on a solid trunk. Above the coat a face – soft, well fed jowls and tired droopy eyes – that speaks both the comforts and the labours of the professional politician.'[8]

On 15 November Ebert's friend Legien, the head of the Socialist trade unions, concluded an agreement with employers, promising to side-step the workers' councils and reject nationalisation of industry in return for union recognition and an eight-hour working day. Capital and labour in partnership, the needs of the economy overcoming political divisions, as Groener had envisaged in 1916. The patriotic compromise that had carried the labour movement through the war reached its culmination: Ebert and Legien placed the fate of the new republic in the hands of the old order – the army command, the state bureaucracy and the industrialists. Ebert saw this as essential to stabilise a shattered Germany and make a safe transition to parliamentary democracy. But as one historian remarks, 'Thus, the solution of an immediate problem was approached by means which incurred a potential danger for the republic in future.'[9]

ooooo

Prince Max had sought an armistice based on the German understanding of President Wilson's Fourteen Points, the vagueness of which left room for interpretation. By the morning of 10 November, when the Allies' armistice terms were before the cabinet in Berlin, Ebert had replaced Prince Max as Chancellor. Ebert's initial hope had been to form a government including the Independents, the Centre, the Progressives and the National Liberals to ensure the burden

Prince Max von Baden

of agreeing the armistice was shared. Persuading the bourgeois parties to work with the Independents had proved impossible. Ebert agreed with the cabinet that the terms were punitive but the military command had approved them and he would take personal responsibility for their acceptance.

Erzberger, the leader of the Centre Party and architect of the 1917 'peace resolution', led the German Armistice Commission. Erzberger and his companions – a Foreign Office official, an army general and a navy captain – went first to military headquarters at Spa. Here Hindenburg told Erzberger he would have to sacrifice himself for the Fatherland.[10] The deputation passed through No Man's Land and across French lines early on 8 November. A train carried them to a railway siding in the forest of Compiègne, north-east of Paris. They were escorted to a coach on the train used as headquarters by the Allied supreme commander, Marshal Ferdinand Foch.

At 9 a.m. Foch entered and read Erzberger the Allied terms, 35 in all, demanding acceptance within 72 hours. Erzberger asked that the army be allowed to retain sufficient strength to suppress Bolshevist revolution, which, he said, if triumphant in Germany would place France in danger. Foch dismissed this, along with Erzberger's request for lifting of the Allied blockade of Germany. No negotiation was possible: Germany could either accept or reject his terms. After a flurry of telegrams to Berlin and military headquarters at Spa, Erzberger and his companions signed the armistice shortly after 5 a.m. on 11 November. Foch, his chief of staff, and the

British First Sea Lord, Admiral Rosslyn Wemyss, signed for the Allies. Fighting would end at 11 a.m. A German officer later recalled, 'The war was entirely lost. As adjutant I had to give the order of the day. On the 11th of November it was: "From noon [German time] onwards our guns will be silent." Four years before, full of optimism, now a beaten army.'[11]

In signing the armistice, Germany accepted responsibility for the war and the principle of reparations: 'Compensation will be made by Germany for all the damages done to the civilian population of the Allies and their property by the aggression of Germany by land, by sea, and from the air.'[12] For France above all, the terms were intended to prevent Germany posing any further threat. German troops were to withdraw from northern France, Belgium, Luxembourg and Alsace-Lorraine within two weeks; demobilisation of the army of six million men was to begin at once. Germany was to evacuate the left bank of the Rhine – which would come under Allied occupation, with Germany meeting the costs – and bridgeheads on the right bank at Cologne, Koblenz and Mainz.

The armed forces were to surrender large quantities of equipment, including 30,000 machine guns, 5,000 artillery pieces and 2,000 aircraft. Germany was also to hand to the Allies 5,000 lorries, 5,000 locomotives and 150,000 railway wagons, all in working condition, in recompense for what the occupying armies had requisitioned. The submarine fleet was to be surrendered, together with the bulk of the surface fleet. The Allies would maintain the naval blockade until Germany signed a formal peace treaty, but would supply food in return for payment in gold or hard currency. Germany was to renounce the Treaties of Brest-Litovsk and Bucharest, made with Russia and Romania earlier in the year, and withdraw behind her eastern frontiers of August 1914. However, German troops on Russian soil were to remain until the Allies authorised withdrawal.

Vorwärts, the SPD newspaper that was effectively Ebert's mouthpiece, commented, 'The conditions of the armistice are very hard, but after the collapse of the former regime the popular government had no other alternative but to accept them. The conditions will be honourably carried out.'[13] The author of the most comprehensive study of the armistice has no doubt that Britain and France achieved their major war aims on 11 November. 'The British wanted the destruction of the German battle fleet, and they wanted the German economy crippled. They achieved both goals, and they removed any threat that Germany might win hegemony on the Continent. The French wanted an end to the German menace, the return of Alsace and Lorraine, and the establishment of the Rhine as a strategic frontier. For the moment, they had all of that.'[14] But disagreements between the Allies and the United States over the armistice conditions foreshadowed the difficulties formulating a final peace would present.

ooooo

Opinion is divided on how far Ebert's actions as Chancellor settled the new republic's ultimate fate from the moment of its birth. The steps he took were consistent with the direction his party had been travelling since at least 1905 and with his own political personality. The problems Ebert's government faced in 1918–19 were immense: concluding a peace treaty after four years of bitter struggle, ensuring an orderly demobilisation of the army, feeding the population against the background of a continuing Allied blockade, overseeing the transition of the country's infrastructure, industry and agriculture from a war to a peacetime economy. As one historian remarks, 'It is hardly surprising, under such circumstances, that the inexperienced Social Democrats felt unequal to the task and were tempted to seek aid from established governmental authorities, even though this might involve risks.' [15] Nothing in Ebert's career or the history of the SPD had prepared them for what they faced in 1918; nothing in Ebert's temperament suggested he was a man to take radical or imaginative action.

For Ebert the choices facing Germany were stark: parliamentary democracy or what he saw as the chaos of a Bolshevik dictatorship. To institute democracy required order and it was for this reason that in the months after 9 November Ebert and his fellow SPD leaders, weighed down by their everyday responsibilities, cast their lot with the pre-existing elites – the military command, the civil service, the industrialists, the judiciary – giving legitimacy to an order exposed by the war as a sham. Not, however, that Ebert was immediately under pressure from the streets for sweeping radicalism. The Independents with whom he shared office sensed that the road to democracy was being undermined, but – riven by their own divisions – lacked the confidence and strength to do more than complain. The more radical Spartacist League, led by Liebknecht and Luxemburg, lacked support and were easily, though wrongly, dismissed as alien Bolshevists. Few in the workers' and soldiers' councils – whose delegates were directly elected but dominated by the SPD and its ideological passivity – saw the councils as organs of proletarian power.

But there existed at least a possibility of breaking the mental hold of the discredited establishment and giving the republic a firmer democratic base. Democracy involves more than elections; it was this deeper democracy from which Ebert – an administrator to his fingertips – instinctively shrank. Hating revolution like sin, he rejected the opportunity for genuine social transformation. But the attitude of the powers with which Germany had to conclude peace had also to be taken into account. Would they have accepted any change that posed a challenge to capitalism?

ooooo

Ebert saw the radical left, in particular the Spartacists who were for the moment attached to the Independents, as the Bolshevist threat to German stability and to the democracy he wished to see. He had said in 1917, *In the future there can only be a constitutional state in Germany. That is the will of the people. The victorious proletariat will not erect government by a class.*[16] In a secret order on 16 November, army supreme headquarters instructed officers to support Ebert, irrespective of their own political views. But Emil Barth, an Independent Socialist member of the Council of People's Commissars, believed dismissing Hindenburg and Groener would symbolise the republic's decisive break with the past. Ebert disagreed, arguing that the generals had promised they would not become involved in counter-revolution. On 6 December there were serious clashes in Berlin between radicals and troops in which 18 demonstrators were killed. As strikes and demonstrations spread through Germany, the SPD and radicals accused one another of betraying the revolution. With Ebert's blessing the army began recruiting a frontier force, ostensibly to defend Germany's eastern and western borders, the forerunners of the Freikorps, which the government would use to suppress the radical left.

Ebert now gave a hostage that would haunt the republic as troops returned to Berlin for demobilisation in accordance with the terms of the November armistice. On 11 December Ebert, accompanied by Scheidemann and Haase, greeted columns of officers and men bearing the red, white and black Imperial colours marching down the Unter den Linden to the Brandenburg Gate. Ebert told the massed ranks, *No enemy has overcome you. Only when the preponderance of our opponents in men and material grew heavier did we give up the struggle, and just because of your heroic courage was it our duty not to demand further useless sacrifices of you. You have borne indescribable sufferings, you have accomplished imperishable and almost superhuman deeds, and you have given year after year incomparable proofs of your unshakeable courage. You have protected the homeland from enemy invasion. You have sheltered your wives, children and parents from flames and the slaughter of war. You have preserved Germany's fields and workshops from devastation and destruction. With the deepest emotion the homeland thanks you for that. You can return with heads erect. Never have men done and suffered more than you.*

No enemy has overcome you. The German army, Ebert was saying, had returned undefeated, clearing the path for the right to claim that it had been 'stabbed in the back'. Hindenburg would first use the expression in testimony to a National Assembly committee in November 1919. Ebert did not criticise the old regime or the war that had brought ruin to Germany, indeed could not for his party had loyally supported both from 4 August 1914. But Ebert looked to the future, saying a new Germany had arisen. *The Socialist Republic will be a commonwealth of Labour. Work is the religion of Socialism. We must work with all our strength if we are not to sink*

No enemy has overcome you ... On 11 December 1918 in Berlin the new
Chancellor Friedrich Ebert welcomed the troops returning from the Front after
the Armistice with these words, opening the way for the 'Stab in the Back' legend
that would seriously damage the reputation of the Weimar Republic.

*to a beggar people. The longed-for hour of peace will soon
strike. The Constituent National Assembly will soon firmly
anchor liberty and the Republic with the unassailable will of
the entire German people.*[17] The troops' commanders swore
oaths of loyalty to the republic for themselves and their men.
By nightfall most soldiers had abandoned their regiments
and returned home, where they transformed themselves into
civilians.

The authority of Ebert's provisional government was based
ultimately, if only in name, on the workers' and soldiers'
councils that had sprung up spontaneously in November
1918. On 16 December an all-German congress of councils,

with delegates elected from across the country, convened in Berlin. The decisions of the congress, although dominated by the SPD, suggested a desire for deeper changes than Ebert and his fellow party leaders were prepared to consider. The delegates passed a resolution calling for the socialisation of major industries, particularly mining, though many agreed with a speaker who said that for the moment there was little to take over. Industrial production in 1919 was hardly more than a third of what it had been in 1913. The congress overwhelmingly supported elections to a constituent National Assembly, in effect an agreement that the upper and middle classes would resume their voice in Germany's government, a parliamentary rather than the proletarian democracy the radicals advocated.

But the delegates were entirely at odds with Ebert in their attitude to the military, setting out their insistence on disarming the danger they posed to a genuinely democratic republic. A seven-point resolution on the 'destruction of militarism and the abolition of blind obedience' demanded a popular militia instead of a standing army, a ban on insignia of rank, the election of officers, and the transfer of supreme military command to the People's Commissars – in effect an abolition of the officer corps that threatened to unravel Ebert's agreement with Groener. On 20 December an agitated Groener met Ebert, threatening that Hindenburg and the entire General Staff would resign if the congress' resolution were not ignored. Ebert took Groener to meet the councils' executive committee, where the general told the delegates that the less they interfered the more quickly order would be established. Ebert persuaded the executive committee that implementing the resolution should be deferred. It was he said, in any case, only to be regarded as guidance rather than an instruction.

The Independents and the Spartacists were incensed at Ebert's continuing submission to the officer corps. On 23 December radical sailors of the People's Naval Division took the military governor of Berlin prisoner in a dispute over pay, holding him in the royal stables. Ebert, to Groener's annoyance, was unwilling to use troops, but on 24 December the Horse Guards moved against the sailors. In a lull in the firing groups of civilians surrounded the attackers, pleading with them to give up the fight. The Horse Guards melted away, many abandoning their weapons. Ebert was left convinced that his government's survival required a more reliable force, the volunteer paramilitary Freikorps of demobilised officers, non-commissioned officers and adventurers. On 29 December the Independents – fragmenting as the left wing split off to form the Communist Party – withdrew their three representatives from the Council of People's Commissars in protest at the use of troops on Christmas Eve, leaving the SPD in sole charge of the government.

The provisional government now took the initiative, dismissing Berlin's radical police commander on 4 January. On the same day Ebert and Noske, defence minister in the new government, inspected a parade of the Freikorps outside the city. 'Just be calm,' Noske told Ebert, 'everything is going to be all right again.' [18] The radicals now walked into the trap Ebert had set. On 5 January, buoyed by massive demonstrations supporting the police commander, the left wing of the Independents, the Revolutionary Shop Stewards and Liebknecht of the new Communist Party set up a revolutionary committee to depose Ebert's government. In what became known as the Spartacist Rising, the radicals seized official buildings in Berlin and the offices of *Vorwärts*.

Noske deployed the Freikorps in Berlin on 11 January,

taking the working-class areas street by street. Hundreds died in the fighting and hundreds more were killed in summary executions that followed. On 15 January Liebknecht and his fellow Communist leader Luxemburg – both pre-war colleagues of Ebert in the SPD – were captured and murdered. As news of the extent of Freikorps brutality spread, Haase – once co-chairman of the SPD with Ebert and only weeks before a member of his government – wrote to his daughter, 'The white terror is raging as it once did under the Tsarist regime ... Disregarding the few legal protective measures, soldiers of the government force their way by night with drawn bayonets into homes ... Landsberg, Ebert, and Scheidemann, who masqueraded as protectors of legality, give full powers to the soldiery... This cannot come to a good end.'[19]

Spartacist Rising in Berlin: radicals seize the offices of Vorwärts, which is heavily damaged in the ensuing fighting.

The events in Berlin were one element in a second revolutionary wave that ran on into the summer, with strikes and risings in central Germany, the industrial Ruhr district, Hamburg, Bremen, Brunswick and Munich, all suppressed by the Freikorps and the army. Ebert told a meeting with state governments on 31 January, *If one has sufficient means of force, then governing is easy; it has been very difficult to create a military force; finally, we have succeeded.*[20] In the midst of the turmoil generated by disappointment with the gains of November, elections had gone ahead on 19 January to the Constituent National Assembly.

The results of the elections – the first in which women were able to vote – came as a disappointment to the SPD, which had based its strategy on democratisation leading to a Socialist majority. The SPD, with 37.9 per cent of the vote, won 165 of the 421 seats. The predominantly Catholic Centre Party took 91 seats, with a little under 20 per cent of the national vote, and the Democrats 75, with 18.5 per cent. The Independents won 7.6 per cent and 22 seats. The parties of the right, the Nationalists and the People's Party, gained 44 and 19 seats respectively. The SPD, the Centre and the Democrats – the parties of the Prince Max coalition – agreed they would form the new government.

> **If one has sufficient means of force, then governing is easy.**
> **EBERT, 31 JANUARY 1919**

Continuing radical activity in Berlin forced the National Assembly to meet in Weimar, which Ebert and Noske agreed was easier to defend than the capital. The deputies gathered in the national theatre at 3 p.m. on 6 February for Ebert's inaugural address. Confidently turning his back on his party's past, he criticised both the old regime and the Allies. *We have lost the war. This fact is not in any way the result of the revolution. It was the Imperial Government of Prince Max of Baden which arranged the armistice which has made us helpless … The revolution declines to accept the responsibility for the misery into which the German people have been plunged by the distorted policy of the ancient regime and the arrogance of militarism.* The Allied blockade, he said, was responsible for the hunger the German people continued to endure. He warned the Allies not to push them too far. *In reliance upon President*

Wilson's 14 points, Germany laid down her arms. Now give us the Wilson peace, to which we have a claim. The Allies, Ebert went on, claimed they had taken up arms against Kaiserism and militarism. The revolution, he said, had ended both. *Militarism has fallen to pieces and will never rise again.*[21]

> 'His enemies prophesy three to six months' tenure of office for him [Ebert]; his friends hope for twelve.'
>
> *THE TIMES*, 14 FEBRUARY 1919

The National Assembly elected Ebert – who according to Scheidemann had already confided, *The Presidency will suit me best*[22] – as head of state on 11 February, a week after his 48th birthday. He said in his acceptance speech that he would act as the representative of the entire German people. *But I declare also that I am a son of the working classes, that I have grown up in the mental environment of Socialism, and that I am not disposed ever to conceal my origin or my convictions.*[23] Scheidemann formed a cabinet two days later comprising SPD, Centre and Democrat members – an alliance (as in the days of the July 1917 'peace resolution' and Prince Max's October 1918 government) between working-class moderates and the liberal-minded middle class. Brockdorff-Rantzau, though attached to no party but whom Ebert and Scheidemann had known and respected as German ambassador in Copenhagen, was appointed foreign minister. A British journalist noted of Ebert, 'His eyes behind his glasses are somehow good-natured. I suppose he is proud of his position, but he does not show it. His manner lacks charm, but he looks and is almost by everybody credited with being, sincere. His enemies prophesy three to six months' tenure of office for him; his friends hope for twelve.'[24]

As the long-awaited Peace Conference in Paris opened, how far Germany could be accused of responsibility for the war was the subject of bitter exchanges in the National Assembly. The Independent Socialists accepted it as a fact, as they had throughout the war. The SPD denied it, in the process defending the discredited Imperial regime. On 25 February Noske objected to an accusation from the Independent Haase that he had a militaristic spirit of conquest that would not have been out of place under the old order. Ebert exploded, *What! Haase still talks about a war of conquest, when it is absolutely established that Germany fought solely to defend her existence.*[25]

II
The Paris Peace Conference

The Signing of Peace in the Hall of Mirrors, Versailles, 28th June 1919
by Sir William Orpen
Front row: Dr Johannes Bell (Germany) signing with Herr Hermann Müller
leaning over him.
Middle row (seated, left to right): President Woodrow Wilson (United States); M
Georges Clemenceau (France); Mr David Lloyd George (Great Britain).
Back row (left to right): Col Sir Maurice Hankey, Mr Edwin S Montagu (Great
Britain); the Maharajah of Bikaner (India).

4

Setting the Terms, 1919

When the guns ceased firing on 11 November 1918, the French prime minister Georges Clemenceau warned, 'We have won the war: now we have to win the peace, and it may be more difficult.' President Wilson had similar fears as he crossed the Atlantic in December, confiding to an aide, 'The picture that keeps coming before me – I hope with all my heart that it is a mistaken foreboding – is of a tragedy of disappointments.'[1] Over four years of war had left a devastated and embittered Europe. France had lost almost a million and a half soldiers, Britain three quarters of a million, Italy 600,000 and Germany two million. Even the United States, which had not entered the conflict until 1917, lost over 100,000 men. To these were added the physically wounded and mentally scarred, the widowed and the orphaned.

Relief that the horror had come to an end was tempered in France and Britain with a determined sense that reparation was due from Germany. Wilson had said in February 1918 that when peace came it should be one of 'no annexations, no contributions, no punitive damages'. The British prime minister, David Lloyd George, expressed a similar sentiment in November. 'We must not allow any sense of revenge, any spirit of greed, any grasping desire, to override the fundamental principles of righteousness.'[2] But a month later, at the tail-end of an election campaign intended to reap a personal victory from the peace, he was demanding the ex-Kaiser's trial. 'There is absolutely no doubt that he has committed a crime against national right. There is absolutely no doubt that he ought to be held responsible for it.' On reparations he said they should be 'up to the limit of [Germany's] capacity'. Then he appeared carried away by his audience's enthusiasm. 'First, as far as justice is concerned, we have an absolute right to demand the whole cost of the war. The second point is that we propose to demand the whole cost of the war.'[3] Voters returned Lloyd George's coalition on 14 December with a substantial majority.

The German Foreign Office waited anxiously during the nine-week hiatus between the armistice and the opening of the Peace Conference in January 1919, preparing arguments for the expected negotiations with the victors. Wilson's arrival in Europe was delayed by congressional mid-term elections in November. His Republican opponents won control of the Senate and the House of Representatives, leaving it uncertain that whatever Wilson put his name to in France would be ratified at home. Wilson arrived at Brest on the USS *George Washington* on 13 December. Finding minimal arrangements had yet been made for the conference, Wilson toured Allied capitals for a month, greeted as the saviour from the New World, before taking up residence at a small house in the Place des États Unis. The British delegation arrived on 11 January, setting up at the Hôtel Majestic on the Avenue Kléber and the adjoining Hôtel Astoria. Lloyd George took a comfortable house on the Rue Nitot.

The Supreme War Council – the heads of government of Britain, France, Italy and the United States – held a preliminary business session of the conference on 12 January at the French foreign office on the Quai d'Orsay. They agreed that Japan would be a side member of the leading body, that the conference's official languages would be English and French and that Clemenceau would chair proceedings. The next day Wilson set out his order of priorities: the establishment of a League of Nations, reparations, the new European states, frontiers and colonies. The peacemakers had treaties to sign with Germany, Austria, Hungary, Bulgaria and Turkey. The German settlement would inevitably dominate but for Wilson the League of Nations was the key element. He wrote to his wife, '[O]nce established, the League can arbitrate and correct mistakes which are inevitable in the treaty we are trying to make at this time.'[4]

> **THE BIG FOUR: BRITAIN, FRANCE, THE UNITED STATES AND ITALY**
> 'The Four bickered, shouted and swore at each other, but they also, even Orlando, teased each other, told jokes, and commiserated with each other. They pored over maps and even crawled together over Wilson's huge map of Europe, which had to be unrolled on the floor. Lloyd George and Wilson talked about going to church; Clemenceau said he had never been in one in his life.'[5]
>
> Margaret MacMillan, *Peacemakers*

Wilson's overall position contrived to be at once precise and hazy, his Fourteen Points – though clearly expressed – lending themselves to a range of interpretations. He believed that all nationalities should have, as far as practicable, self-determination; that all states should reduce their armies and armaments; that there should be no more secret diplomacy, no treaties negotiated by politicians behind the people's backs. Above all, he believed the civilised world should work as a community in the League of Nations to prevent disputes descending into the savagery of war. He wanted little for the United States, having no fears for his country's security. As far as economics were concerned, the Fourteen Points had mentioned only free trade, a liberal principle certainly, and one that would benefit the world's leading industrial power.

Wilson was by no means the starry-eyed idealist Lloyd George and Clemenceau feared. In 1915 he had despatched the Marines to Haiti, making the country an American protectorate. The following year he sent troops to the Dominican Republic to prop up a dictatorship friendly to American business interests. To that extent, Ebert had been accurate when he told Prince Max in October 1918 that Wilson was *still an imperialist*. In addition, Wilson had no feel for the complexities of Europe and grasped little of the First World War's tangled origins, certain only that Germany had been at fault in breaching Belgian neutrality and that she had to pay a price for that. But Wilson had specifically said when the United States declared war in April 1917 that the enemy was the government of the German Empire and this gave the new administration in Berlin some hope.

For Britain, Lloyd George was steeped in the background to the war and had lived through its daily grind, but he had now manoeuvred himself into a dangerously ambiguous position, one in which the desires for peace and for retribution conflicted. As Clemenceau was never slow to remind him, Britain had already achieved her major objectives – the removal of the threat posed by the German navy, in particular submarines, and her merchant fleet, and the British Empire had captured most of Germany's colonies. But Germany had been one of Britain's major trading partners before 1914, as both customer and supplier. It was in Britain's interest that

Germany should not be dealt such a crushing economic blow that she would be unable eventually to resume that position or so politically humiliated as to persuade her to throw in her lot with Bolshevism. Though France had been Britain's wartime ally, Lloyd George now sought a balance between the two leading continental powers, wary of either dominating. But he had given hostages to fortune in the general election campaign, leading the British public to expect the Kaiser would be punished for war crimes and that Germany would be forced to make substantial reparation.

France's main concerns were security and reparations. Twice in half a century she had been invaded by Germany, a neighbour surpassing her in population, industrial power and – until 1918 – military might. The north-east of France had been occupied and ravaged for four years. Now Germany was on her knees, Clemenceau intended to keep her there for the foreseeable future. He was determined Germany should be deprived of territory in the west – Alsace-Lorraine certainly, hopefully the Rhineland (possibly as an independent but French-dominated buffer state) and the coal-rich Saar. In the east, Poland should be reborn at Germany's expense, while the smaller states emerging from Austria-Hungary's collapse would become France's allies. Germany would be contained, would pay for the costs of the war and the damage she had inflicted and be so disarmed that she would never be in the position to threaten another. His view of the way the conference should be conducted was uncomplicated: 'You must never negotiate with a German or conciliate him; you must dictate to him.'[6]

The Italian prime minister, Vittorio Orlando, carried least weight in this 'Big Four', speaking no English and taking an interest only when issues directly concerning his country were involved. Italy had originally been part of the Triple Alliance with Germany and Austria-Hungary but had been persuaded to enter the war on the Allied side in 1915 with promises of substantial territorial gains. When it became obvious that Italy would not be making those gains he withdrew, re-appearing only for the signing ceremony.

One substantial party was missing – the Germans. In November 1918 Wilson's close aide, Edward House, had allocated five seats for a German delegation at the forthcoming conference. According to a member of the British delegation it remained uncertain from January to March 1919 whether the victors were hammering out preliminary terms to present to Germany for discussion or were producing the final article. 'In fact the problem was shelved throughout that period as something which was too painful to raise immediately, as something which would settle itself.'[7] Given the differences among the Allies, a German presence would have been politically embarrassing, enabling the Germans to play off one ally against the other. But until almost the last moment the Germans expected negotiations and were formulating arguments to counter the positions they calculated the Allies would take.

When the National Assembly had met for its inaugural session in Weimar on 6 February 1919 Ebert had outlined the position a German delegation would take. What was revealing was that Ebert felt able to complain about the treaty before it had even been written. He said the Allies claimed they took up arms against the Prussian militarism epitomised by the Kaiser; both had gone. He rejected German guilt for the war and Britain and France's expectation that Germany would pay

> **The German people cannot be made the paid slaves of other countries for 20, 40, or 60 years.**
> EBERT, 6 FEBRUARY 1919

indemnities. *These plans for revenge and domination call for the sharpest protest. The German people cannot be made the paid slaves of other countries for 20, 40, or 60 years ... In view of the stupendous misery of the peoples, in view of the stupendous misery on all sides, the question of guilt seems to be almost trifling. Nevertheless the German people are resolved to call to account themselves all those against whom intentional guilt or malicious action can be proved. But those ought not to be punished who were themselves victims, victims of the war, victims of our former lack of freedom.*[8] In an interview a week later Ebert said Germany's delegates would go to Paris with a definite programme and take a lively part in negotiations. They would not submit tamely to being dictated to.

The newly appointed foreign minister, Count Ulrich von Brockdorff-Rantzau, took a similar line in the National Assembly on 14 February. He said it was too soon to allocate responsibility for the war, which should be determined by an impartial judge, not by the victors acting as both prosecutor and jury. He recognised that Germany would lose territory, but insisted the inhabitants should make their own choice in accord with Wilson's principle of national self-determination. Germany was perfectly willing to disarm, provided the Allies and Germany's neighbours did. Subsequent Foreign Office memoranda reiterated Germany's willingness to pay for damage her troops had caused in the occupied territories, but not the total cost of the war.

ooooo

The 32 delegations that convened in Paris for the first formal session on 18 January 1919 were not concerned solely with

Germany, though that country's fate would dominate proceedings. The leaders, representing 75 per cent of the world's
population, were there to recast the globe. Wilson had first
hoped that the full plenary conference would constitute the
power-house of decision, wanting to avoid behind-the-scenes
manipulation by a few powerful personalities, the unaccount-
able plotting he believed had led to the war. But the numbers
involved and the range of issues made this impracticable; the
full conference met only a dozen times. In practice the great
powers dominated, first in a Council of Ten comprising the
heads of government and foreign ministers of the United
States, Britain, France, Italy and Japan. By March this too
proved unworkable as conflicts of interest over central issues
became more apparent. A Council of Four – Wilson, Lloyd
George, Clemenceau and, until he returned to Rome in disappointment, Orlando – now met daily to argue out matters
and to contrive a common front. Below the Council of Four
and a Council of Foreign Ministers were over 50 advisory
committees.

While the committees undertook technical studies and
drafted sections of the treaties, discussion was dominated by
face-to-face contact between the leading personalities. One
historian of Versailles describes their individual characteristics: 'Clemenceau ... spoke with emphasis and precision,
bent on attaining his end with the least possible delay; Lloyd
George in a bewildering stream of words, full of esprit, not
disdaining the use of little witticisms when he was not in a
pugnacious mood; Wilson very slowly, with conscious dignity
in every word, often gazing fixedly into the far distance;
Orlando hardly at all.'[9]

Both Clemenceau and Lloyd George were irritated by Wilson's insistence that drafting the Covenant of the League

of Nations should precede the formulation of peace terms. Wilson was determined that work on the Covenant should be completed by 15 February, when he had to return to Washington to spend a month completing Congressional business. On 14 February he read the draft Covenant to the conference plenary session, a compromise between his hope of a 'league of democracies' and Clemenceau's desire for a military alliance against aggression. The conference accepted the draft for study and Wilson left the following day for the United States, where he found growing isolationist sentiment resented the extent of the obligations the Covenant implied.

With Wilson away, Lloyd George returned to London. On 19 February Clemenceau was shot in the street by an anarchist, a bullet lodging by his lung. Substantive work on the peace treaties did not begin in earnest until Wilson returned on 14 March and Clemenceau's convalescence was complete. Full attention could now be devoted to formulating terms for treaties with Germany's allies – Austria, Hungary, Bulgaria and Turkey – but, above all, Germany herself. The four leaders agreed to establish the Council of Four as the chief committee of the conference, Japan's objections to her exclusion were ignored. This 'Big Four' usually met in the library at Wilson's residence, arguing bitterly on some occasions, on others recognising with the fellow feeling of elected politicians a shared precariousness.

At one tempestuous session, Clemenceau accused Wilson of being pro-German and of caring nothing for France's security. A furious Wilson threatened to leave Paris at once. Clemenceau said that was not what he wanted, and then walked out of the meeting. On the afternoon Wilson arrived back in Paris, he and Lloyd George agreed to offer France a military guarantee against German aggression. Clemenceau refused to respond at once but on 18 March demanded Allied occupation of the Rhineland. Through 145 meetings from March to May, argument raged over the major issues: the disposal of Germany's colonies, her borders, disarmament and, most contested of all, reparations.

As the details were thrashed out, Lloyd George revealed a growing concern about the dangers of pressing Germany too far. He put his thoughts in a document entitled 'Some Considerations for the Peace Conference before they finally draft their Terms', composed at Fontainebleau outside Paris and presented to his 'Big Four' colleagues on 25 March. He said the Allies must present Germany with terms she was capable of meeting, including those dealing with reparations. The alternatives were the indefinite deployment of a large army of occupation to enforce fulfilment or Germany throwing in her lot with Bolshevik Russia. 'Once that happens all Eastern Europe will be swept into the orbit of the Bolshevik revolution and within a year we may witness the spectacle of nearly three hundred million people organised into a vast red army under German instructors and German generals equipped with German cannon and German machine guns and prepared for a renewal of the attack on Western Europe.'[11] Lloyd George argued that as few Germans as possible should be placed under non-German rule and Germany should be admitted to the League of Nations on signing the peace. Clemenceau reacted scathingly. He said France agreed on the need for a just peace but he was not sure that Germany and the Allies

'You may strip Germany of her colonies, reduce her armaments to a mere police force and her army to that of a fifth-rate power; all the same in the end if she feels that she has been unjustly treated in the peace of 1919 she will find means of exacting retribution from her conquerors.' Lloyd George, Fontainebleau Memorandum, 25 March 1919.[10]

saw justice in the same terms. The reaction in Britain was as critical. On 8 April 200 MPs sent a telegram to Lloyd George in Paris expressing anxiety that he appeared to be weakening in the demands he was making on Britain's behalf.

The simplest issue appeared to be the disbursement of Germany's colonies. Lloyd George had first raised this in the Council of Ten at the end of January, under pressure from the white Dominions of South Africa, New Zealand and Australia, who had seized German territories, and bound by promises Britain had made to Italy and Japan in secret wartime treaties. There was no dispute that Germany would not regain her colonies, but Wilson held out against outright annexation – which he thought was hardly an auspicious beginning for the League of Nations – and believed the inhabitants' wishes should be taken into account. Working with the South African representative, Jan Smuts, Lloyd George came up with a compromise formula of 'mandates' under the League of Nations. The victorious powers would hold what they had conquered in trust, overseeing their development. However, it was not until 6 May that final agreement was reached on the sharing out of Germany's former colonies in Africa and Asia, annexation in all but name.

Germany's western and eastern frontiers proved more contentious. That Alsace-Lorraine would return to French control was unquestioned and Belgium would also be compensated with small packets of territory for losses she had sustained in the war. But France sought a far more weakened Germany in the west, one that would prevent any future attack. 'If we are not on the Rhine, everything is lost,' Marshal Foch reportedly said as the conference opened.[12] Clemenceau suggested in a memorandum of 25 February that Germany's frontier should be pulled back to the Rhine and that the Allies should permanently garrison troops at the bridge-heads. France briefly encouraged separatist sentiment in the area, believing an independent Rhineland would remove the 'Prussian' threat. This came to nothing. France also sought the Saar, an area rich in coal. Lloyd George agreed with this demand; Wilson was against. But Wilson and Lloyd George were in accord over the Rhineland – to transfer the terri-tory to France would replicate Germany's seizure of Alsace-Lorraine in 1871 and guarantee another war. The 'Big Four' agreed that Allied troops would occupy the Rhineland and its bridgeheads for 15 years and that France would have sole access to the Saar's coalfields for the same period. Britain and the United States would also give France a permanent mili-tary guarantee against Germany. In the event, the guarantee came to nothing when the United States' Senate refused to ratify the treaty.

Difficult as settlement in the west had been, Germany's eastern frontiers presented even more complexities and would in the long run pose the greatest threat to European peace. New states had arisen in the east with the collapse of the empires of Russia, Germany and Austria-Hungary – Czechoslovakia, Hungary and a revived Poland. The emer-gence of Poland affected Germany most. The thirteenth of Wilson's Fourteen Points had stated, 'an independent Polish state should be erected which should include the territories inhabited by indisputably Polish populations, which should be assured a free and secure access to the sea …'. The leader of the Polish delegation at the conference demanded on 29 January that her borders should return to what they had been when the country was first partitioned in 1772, that ter-ritory in Upper Silesia (lost in the 14th century) should be returned and that Poland should have the port of Danzig and access to it by detaching parts of East and West Prussia from Germany.

When a commission appointed by the Council supported the bulk of Poland's demands on 19 March, Wilson and Clemenceau agreed. Lloyd George pointed out that doing so would place substantial numbers of German nationals under Polish rule. He presented arguments against the commission's recommendations, gaining small changes. When the draft treaty was finalised Germany was to lose the 'Polish corridor', Danzig was to be a free port under League of Nations control, while the fates of other areas were to be decided by plebiscite.

There were similar difficulties over the Sudetenland, an area of the new Czechoslovakia formerly ruled by Austria-Hungary, whose inhabitants were culturally and linguistically German. France was determined the area should not go to Germany (though the principle of national self-determination implied otherwise) and Lloyd George seemingly showed little awareness that there was a problem. The decision was made almost in passing on 4 April that the Sudeten Germans would come under Czechoslovak rule. On a separate issue of self-determination, Britain and America had no real objection to a union of Austria with Germany, but France's strenuous objections to the enemy emerging from the war more powerful prevailed.

On 13 February Marshal Foch, who had drafted the November 1918 armistice terms, was put at the head of the commission on the future of Germany's armed forces. The objective was to ensure Germany was denied the means to wage aggressive war again. The commission proposed on 3 March that Germany should have a 200,000-strong conscript army, with 9,000 volunteer officers. The French argued for a smaller force of 100,000, all conscripts. Britain and the United States preferred a volunteer force, Lloyd George declaring he saw conscription as the source of militarism. After Wilson's return on 14 March there was compromise agreement on a volunteer army of 100,000. Germany was to be forbidden to deploy troops or maintain fortifications on the west bank of the Rhine or to have a military general staff or an air force.

The problem of Germany's fleet – interned by Britain in the Orkneys – proved less easy to resolve, Lloyd George and Wilson wanting to see it destroyed, Clemenceau and Orlando hoping to augment their own navies by sharing it out. The fleet settled the matter by scuttling itself, all 400,000 tons, on 21 June. It was agreed that strict limitations would be imposed on Germany's future navy, with an absolute ban on submarines. By 17 March all issues of German disarmament had been resolved. Wilson's hope was that the reduction in German forces would be a preliminary to a world-wide cutback in armaments and armies.

The final and most intractable issue was that of reparations. Britain and France had no doubt of their entitlement to reparations from Germany, but both were concerned that the demand should at least appear legally watertight. Two members of the American delegation found a form of words: Germany and her allies were to acknowledge moral responsibility for the loss and damage their aggression had caused, which would be translated into a financial obligation. But if the war had been a crime, how should the Allies deal with the criminals themselves? Wilson agreed, with some reluctance, that a commission would determine the causes of the war, identify those responsible and punish them. It was agreed, though not without some misgivings, that the ex-Kaiser should stand trial before an international court.

The divisions between the United States on one hand and Britain and France on the other as to what constituted adequate reparations were wide. The United States wanted nothing for herself and Wilson sought to confine Germany's obligations to two categories: violations of international law through the breach of Belgian neutrality and the illegal treatment of prisoners, and damage and loss incurred by the Allies' civilian populations. But Wilson did expect the Allies to repay what they had borrowed from the United States to fight the war, introducing another complexity into the argument. Britain owed the United States $4.7 billion and France $4 billion. France owed Britain a further $3 billion, while both had made loans to Russia that they doubted they would ever see repaid.

Lloyd George had initially taken a brutal view, telling his cabinet, 'Somebody had to pay. If Germany could not pay, it meant the British taxpayer had to pay. Those who ought to pay were those who caused the loss.'[13] British public opinion, which Lloyd George had whipped up in the 1918 general election, wanted the entire costs of the war squeezed out of Germany. But he was equally aware that Britain's post-war economic recovery depended on Germany's ability to buy her imports. However, if Wilson's view prevailed, Britain, which had spent most on the war but had suffered less civilian damage than France or Belgium, would have a small share in reparation. It was therefore necessary for him to push for a wider interpretation of civilian loss and damage. Clemenceau was under similar pressure. His position was that Germany should pay for the restoration of the territory they had occupied in northern France and repay French war debts. Less dependent on trade with Germany, he saw an advantage for France in keeping Germany economically weak. His strategy was, however, more subtle. He sought to convince Wilson that, although Germany would find it difficult if not impossible to meet the full extent of France's claim, he should recognise its justice. In this way the United States would be drawn into helping France meet the costs she had incurred in fighting the war.

On 25 January 1919 the conference set up a Commission on the Reparation of Damage, with three representatives from each of the major powers, two each from the smaller. The commission successfully identified the central problems but was hard put to find a solution. By mid-February, when Wilson returned to Washington, Britain was demanding a payment of £24 billion and France £44 billion, both stretching the concept of 'civilian' loss and damage to include pensions for disabled soldiers, widows, orphans and the costs of reconstruction. The Americans were suggesting that Germany should pay a far smaller amount, £4.4 billion in all. The Americans proposed that a specific figure should be included in the treaty; the British and French opposed this, arguing that it would take at least a year to calculate the damage in Belgium and northern France, but also aware that any definite amount would arouse angry disappointment at home.

The deadlock was still unbroken when Wilson returned to Paris in March, as it proved impossible to arrive at a figure that would satisfy Allied public opinion while appearing realistic to Germany. Even Lloyd George, as the Fontainebleau memorandum showed, was beginning to doubt the wisdom of imposing too great a burden on the Germans. On 5 April the 'Big Four' agreed that Germany should at least make an interim payment. Two days later they kicked the argument into the future with some relief by asking the Reparation Commission to assess damages in detail and present the bill to Germany in May 1921.

ooooo

On 13 April the Big Four gave instructions for Germany to be invited to receive the terms of the treaty. Final, hurried drafting went on until almost the last moment. On 15 April a Committee for Peace Negotiations set up by the German National Assembly met for the first time, expecting that the delegation would be allowed to discuss the treaty's provisions. The German Foreign Office had made a number of assumptions about the terms the Allies might present and had prepared their arguments accordingly. Alsace-Lorraine would, of course, have to be returned to France, but Germany would seek a plebiscite. There would be a dispute over the Saar, which France wanted. Similarly, there would be an argument about ceding Upper Silesia to Poland, which the Foreign Office felt confident of winning. The Allies would deny Germany union with Austria because of French objections, though Italy might support Germany. The Foreign Office believed the conference had ruled against annexing Germany's colonies, but even if they were taken thought their value could be offset against reparations. Reparations themselves would be 50 billion marks at the most, payable over a long period. Germany would accept demilitarisation of the Rhineland and limits on her armed forces.

Germany would, the Foreign Office assumed, be admitted to the League of Nations on signing the treaty, and it prepared three arguments for the delegation: first, Germany would accept nothing that did not accord with Wilson's Fourteen Points; second, as the Allies claimed they had fought against the Kaiser and militarism, it would be wrong now to punish the German people for crimes of which they were innocent; third, the Republic had saved Germany from Bolshevism and

'I HAVE REALLY BEEN DEAD EVER SINCE VERSAILLES.'
Ulrich Graf von Brockdorff-Rantzau (1869–1928). Born into an
aristocratic family with close connections to the Imperial Court and
adopted by his uncle on his father's death, Brockdorff-Rantzau studied
law before joining the army in 1891. Invalided out in 1893 he entered
the diplomatic service, serving in St Petersburg, Vienna and Budapest.
In 1912 he was appointed ambassador to Denmark. During the First
World War he worked to maintain Danish neutrality and ensure food
supplies to Germany, and opposed the adoption of a policy of
unrestricted U-boat warfare in 1917. He was involved in facilitating the
passage of Lenin from Switzerland to Russia in 1917, which ended the
war on the Eastern Front. Sympathetic to liberal reform, he became
close to Ebert and other SPD leaders while maintaining his essentially
conservative views. He declined appointment as Foreign Minister in
1917, wary of the growing dominance of the military in German politics.
A member of the post-revolutionary government in 1918, Brockdorff-
Rantzau became Foreign Minister in February 1919, telling the National
Assembly, 'I hope to give proof that it is possible to be both a count
and a democrat.' He was leader of the German delegation to the Peace
Conference in Versailles, expecting that his role would be one of
negotiating a peace of reconciliation based on President Wilson's
Fourteen Points. Unable to secure worthwhile concessions from the
Allies and unwilling to accept that Germany's responsibility for the war,
he advised the German government to refuse to sign the treaty,
resigning from the government on 20 June. In 1922 Brockdorff-Rantzau
became Germany's first ambassador to the Soviet Union, developing
the close relations between the two outsider powers symbolised by the
Treaty of Rapallo and the 1926 Treaty of Berlin. His final words to his
brother in 1928 were, 'Do not mourn. After all, I have really been dead
ever since Versailles.' [14]

the new Germany represented a barrier for Europe against
its spread.

The five-strong German delegation, led by Brockdorff-
Rantzau, left Berlin on 28 April, accompanied by 180 civil
servants, interpreters, typists and messengers in three trains.
The trains crossed the border, passing through the areas
of greatest devastation in Belgium and northern France. A

German journalist accompanying the party later wrote, 'We were being rehearsed in the penitential roles for which we had already been cast.'[15] Arriving at Versailles station, the delegates were taken by car to the Hôtel des Réservoirs, where their luggage was piled in the courtyard. A French officer ordered soldiers escorting them not to help them shift the bags. The delegates presented their credentials in a brief ceremony at the Trianon Palace on 1 May. 'Brockdorff-Rantzau was pale and nervous – trembling in every limb,' a British diplomat noted in his diary.[16]

It was not until Brockdorff-Rantzau read the agenda for the 7 May session of the conference that he finally understood there was to be no discussion of the terms. Germany's representatives would be expected, the agenda said, to present written observations in English and French within 15 days. There were already misgivings about the treaty among some in the British and American parties. Wilson told a journalist on 6 May, 'If I were a German, I think I should never sign it.' Robert Lansing, the American Secretary of State who had been in Paris throughout, noted, 'The terms of peace appear immeasurably harsh and humiliating, while many of them seem to me impossible of performance.'[17]

The German delegation entered the already full conference hall at the Trianon Palace at 3 p.m. on 7 May, taking their seats at a table opposite the Allied representatives. Clemenceau directly faced the Germans, the Americans to his right, the British to his left. The French prime minister opened the proceedings, presented the treaty and explained the procedure in few words, abrupt and to the point (see Preface). Brockdorff-Rantzau had taken two speeches to the palace, one long and one short, unsure of which to deliver. Clemenceau's attitude decided him to deliver the longer and more defiant. He denied that Germany had been guilty of causing the war, accepted many unjust things had occurred in its course, though Germany had not been alone in that. He said the delegation would study the document carefully but warned, 'A peace which cannot be defended before the world as a peace of justice would always evoke new resistance. No one could sign it with a clear conscience, for it could not be carried out.' [18]

Brockdorff-Rantzau's performance appalled the Allied leaders. Wilson said shortly after: 'This is the most tactless speech I have ever heard. It will set the whole world against them.'[19] Clemenceau had spoken standing; the German Foreign Minister remained seated. An observer close to the action reported, 'Clemenceau impatiently tapped the table with an ivory paper-knife. President Wilson impatiently toyed with a pencil. Lloyd George pressed his paper-knife on the table with such vigour that it broke.' [20] Brockdorff-Rantzau subsequently explained that he had meant no insult; the document he had to read was lengthy and he found it easier to see sitting down.

At the Hôtel des Réservoirs interpreters worked through the night, translating the treaty from English and French into German. On the evening of 8 May the delegates and their specialist advisers gathered after dinner, aghast at what the terms would mean for Germany. Each bewailed the economic and political impact on the young Republic – the burden of reparations, the losses of territory and colonies. As the clamour rose a journalist came in to say every word could be heard outside through the open windows. Brockdorff-Rantzau replied bitterly that he did not care, everyone should know how unanimously the delegation rejected the Allied imposition. Only one of the party, a socialist minister from Saxony, could muster any optimism. 'It may be that the consequences of this Treaty will keep us down for twenty – even twenty-five years – but sooner or later we shall rise. What are twenty-five years in the life of a people?' [21]

The reaction in Germany was less stoical, disappointment turning to anger. Throughout May Ebert and Scheidemann denounced the treaty and demonstrations swept the country. Scheidemann said the German delegation would take every opportunity open to have the terms modified. In the National Assembly on 12 May Scheidemann, from the left, made his famous remark, 'What hand would not wither that binds itself and us in these fetters?' and Gustav Stresemann of the right-wing People's Party agreed. 'This offer is a mixed grill of French vengeance and English brutality.' On 18 May Ebert told a crowd at a rally in the Lustgarten, *Foreign countries will not permit the proscription of Germany. They will raise their voices with us and this peace of enslavement, which we will never sign, shall not come to pass.* [22] But three days later 200,000 thronged the Berlin streets at an Independent Socialist demonstration demanding that Germany should accept the terms. Ebert repeated at a cabinet meeting on 3 and 4 June that the terms remained unacceptable.

> This peace of enslavement, which we will never sign, shall not come to pass.
>
> EBERT, 18 MAY 1919

The German delegation at Versailles had, meanwhile, been sending the Allies notes on specific aspects of the draft treaty, the Allies replying to each that they could accept no alteration. On 20 May the delegation asked for the deadline for comments to be extended. The Allies agreed to give until 29 May. On that day Brockdorff-Rantzau wrote to the Allies, enclosing detailed objections almost as bulky as the treaty itself. He said in a covering letter, 'We expected the Peace of Right which had been promised to us. We were grieved when we read this document to see what conditions victorious Might demanded of us ... The demands of that Treaty are beyond the strength of the German people.' [23] Germany took each of the treaty's terms apart, analysing them, criticising them in almost every case for failing to accord with Wilson's Fourteen Points, the basis on which Germany had sued for peace. The effect was not what Brockdorff-Rantzau had hoped. Wilson, aware how far he had moved from his speeches of 1918, felt pushed into a corner and refused to relent. Clemenceau was confirmed in his view that Germany would take advantage of any sign of weakness.

Only Lloyd George considered the Germans had raised reasonable objections and that concessions were warranted. He asked that Germany should be admitted to the League of Nations, that the occupation of the Rhineland should be briefer, that the drawing of her eastern frontiers should be modified. On just one major point would his colleagues move: there would be a plebiscite before Upper Silesia was transferred to Poland and Germany would be guaranteed supplies of coal from the area. There were other minor modifications. The Allies communicated these concessions to the German delegation on 16 June and gave them five days to accept or reject the revised treaty. The following day Brockdorff-Rantzau and his party left Paris. As their cars left the hotel they were attacked by stone-throwing partisans of the Ligue des Patriots. Several delegates were injured by flying glass.

Brockdorff-Rantzau believed Germany had nothing to lose by delay. He told the cabinet on 19 June, 'If we can hold out for two or three months, our enemies will be at loggerheads over the division of the spoils, and then we shall get better terms

… If we refuse to sign, we shall be in purgatory for a time, for two or at most three months. If we sign, it means a lingering disease, of which the nation will perish.'[24] Ebert wavered as the cabinet divided, at first strongly against signing, then less sure. On 20 June Scheidemann resigned, adamant that Germany should not sign, with half the cabinet equally determined. On 23 June, with a new government installed, the National Assembly voted to accept the treaty by 237 votes to 138 (with five abstentions), with the proviso that the articles (the 'points of honour') on war guilt and the surrender of the former Kaiser and other alleged war criminals were removed. The resolution also asked that the treaty should be revised by the League of Nations within two years of signing. The Allies refused the German conditions, demanding a clear decision, Yes or No, by seven that evening. Forty-two British, French, Belgian and American divisions stood ready to end the armistice and advance into Germany if the answer was No.

5
Signing the Peace, 1919

There are two versions of how the German government reached the final decision to sign the treaty on 23 June 1919. Both emphasise the role of Ebert as Reich President. In the first, Ebert, as in November 1918, turned to the army command for support. He telephoned general headquarters and spoke to Groener, asking for Hindenburg. Ebert said that if the army considered it could defend Germany he would reject the treaty; otherwise there was no choice but to sign. He told Groener he would call again for Hindenburg's opinion. Hindenburg agreed with Groener that resistance was impossible, but when Ebert called again refused to speak to him, preferring his subordinate to shoulder the burden. Groener told Ebert, 'Not as Quartermaster-General, Herr Reich President, but as a German with a clear view of the situation as a whole, I feel it incumbent on me at this hour to give you the following advice: Resumption of the struggle is ultimately hopeless, apart from temporary successes in the East. Peace must therefore be concluded on the terms set by the enemy.'[1] In the second version of events Groener gave his opinion by telegram.

Having ascertained the army command's views, Ebert held a succession of meetings with leaders of the main parties through the day on 23 June. The German National People's party were still reluctant to accept the terms. Ebert asked their leader whether he was prepared to form a government to continue the war. He did not answer. The National Assembly finally agreed there was no choice but to sign the treaty as it stood, the right-wing Nationalists – who continued to oppose this – agreeing that all were acting from patriotic motives. Minutes before the Allied ultimatum expired, the government sent a telegram to Paris reluctantly agreeing to the terms. 'Yielding to overpowering might, the government of the German Republic declares itself ready to accept and to sign the treaty imposed by the Allied and Associated governments. But in so doing, the government of the German Republic in no wise abandons its conviction that these conditions of peace represent injustice without example.' [2] The telegram was taken to Wilson, Clemenceau and Lloyd George, who were meeting in Wilson's study, 90 minutes before Allied troops were to resume hostilities against Germany.

> 'The government of the German Republic in no wise abandons its conviction that these conditions of peace represent injustice without example.'
> **GERMAN TELEGRAM TO THE ALLIES, 23 JUNE 1919**

On the following day, 24 June, Ebert appealed to the German people to work to fulfil the treaty's conditions, leaving a proviso. *So far as it is possible to carry it into effect, it must be carried into effect.* He spoke specifically to the army and civil service, as much the pillars of the new regime as of the old. *As, notwithstanding all constraints of conscience, we have remained at our post, so must everyone separately do his best, soldier and peasant, officers, non-commissioned officers and men, and officials – each one must continue faithfully to fulfil his duty in this most evil of all evil days.* But giving the appearance of attempting to fulfil the terms of the treaty was, Ebert and the government made plain, intended to overcome them. If every German did not help, *We shall then have no ameliorations, no revisions, and no final removal of the gigantic burden.* The SPD newspaper, *Vorwärts*, adopted a more defiant tone. 'We shall not rest until this infamous document which defiles every concept of honour and decency lies torn and scattered on the ground. Wilson and Lloyd George may celebrate their tawdry triumph, but we shall bide our time.'[3]

The cabinet met on 26 June to select a fresh delegation to attend Versailles for the signing ceremony. Ebert's long-time friend Hermann Müller, who had been appointed Foreign Minister on Brockdorff-Rantzau's resignation, considered it his duty to undertake what he said was a difficult mission. He asked that a representative of the Social Democrats' major partner in the coalition government, the Centre, should accompany him. Erzberger, who had formulated the July 1917 'peace resolution' and had signed the armistice, refused, saying he was unpopular enough already. The cabinet agreed on Johannes Bell, the colonies minister, who was absent in Essen. Contacted by telephone, he refused, saying he could not, as minister for the colonies, sign a treaty that relinquished them. Ebert telephoned Bell again, pleading that he should go; the Allies were demanding the names of Germany's delegates and the country was in peril. Bell agreed to share the burden with Müller. The cabinet was careful to record in a memorandum the unpleasantness of the duty it had imposed on Müller and Bell. 'They believe it to be impossible to avoid this last and personally most difficult sacrifice, made necessary by the terrible suffering ... which would result from a failure to sign.'[4]

When Müller returned to the Foreign Office, his senior officials openly disagreed with the decision the politicians had reached. Müller subsequently said, 'I could well understand their attitude; but when I attempted to recruit a small staff to accompany my mission to Versailles, each of them begged me insistently not to include him.'[5] The Foreign Minister was able to rally only a small group of four to travel with him and Bell to Versailles. A few hours before, Ebert had called Müller to his office. He found the Reich President in consultation with Bethmann-Hollweg, the Imperial Chancellor on the outbreak of war in 1914. Bethmann-Hollweg had prepared a statement to be given to Clemenceau declaring his willingness to attend any tribunal the Allies convened as a substitute for the ex-Kaiser. In a last loyal gesture to the old regime, Bethmann-Hollweg said that as Chancellor he had been solely responsible for German policy in the days leading up to the war. Ebert and Müller promised the statement would be passed to Clemenceau.

ooooo

What had the Germans agreed to accept, or – as many saw it – had dictated to them?[6] Under the terms of the treaty, Germany lost 13 per cent of her territory, approximately 25,000 square miles, and a little over 10 per cent of her population, around six million. Most of the lost land went to Poland. Two million Germans would be outside her borders; in 1914 there had been four million non-Germans within her frontiers. Germany lost 15 per cent of her agricultural production and 20 per cent of her coal, iron and steel.

THE GERMAN SIGNATORIES AT VERSAILLES

Hermann Müller (1876-1931). Son of a wine producer, Müller joined the SPD in 1893. He was editor of a party newspaper and member of the council in Görlitz from 1903–6, when he was appointed to the SPD executive in Berlin, taking responsibility for relations with European socialist parties. On the eve of the First World War, Müller was dispatched to Paris to discover whether the French socialists would support their government. Elected as a Reichstag deputy in 1916, he was chosen as a member of the executive council of the Berlin Workers' and Soldiers' Councils in November 1918. Müller was elected to the National Assembly in January 1919, became the SPD joint-chairman and was appointed foreign minister on 21 June. He signed the Treaty of Versailles a week later, considering it his painful duty as foreign minister. He was briefly Reich Chancellor in the 'Weimar Coalition' government from March-June 1920. He remained prominent in the SPD, publishing *The November Revolution* in 1928. In June of that year he became Chancellor of a 'Grand Coalition' of the SPD, the Centre, the Democrats and the People's Party, which negotiated the Young Plan on reducing Germany's reparations payments and increased spending on the navy. His administration collapsed in March 1930 as the world depression took hold and the coalition divided over financing unemployment benefit payments. His resignation marked the beginning of the end of Weimar democracy. Müller continued to lead the SPD in the Reichstag until his death following an operation in 1931.

Johannes Bell (1868–1949). Son of an engineer, Bell worked as a lawyer and notary before his election to the Prussian lower house in 1908 as a Centre Party deputy. In 1912 he was elected to the Reichstag. He was a supporter of the July 1917 'peace resolution'. Appointed minister for the colonies in February 1919, Bell was additionally made transport minister in June, holding both posts until 1920. On 26 June 1919 Bell reluctantly agreed to accompany Müller to Versailles as co-signatory to the peace treaty. After Germany's loss of her colonies at Versailles Bell supported campaigns for their restoration. Vice-president of the Reichstag from 1920–6, Bell was minister of justice and minister for the occupied territories from 1926–7. He retired from active politics when the Nazis assumed power in 1933.

In the west, Alsace-Lorraine (seized by the young German Empire in 1871) was restored to France outright (Article 51), without the plebiscite Germany had hoped for. France was compensated for the German destruction of her mines in the Pas de Calais by exclusive access to coalmines in the Saar region (Article 45). The area was to be administered by the League of Nations for 15 years, at which point the population would choose whether they were French or German (Article 49). If they chose to be German, France would receive financial compensation for losing the mines. Moresnet, a small area hitherto under joint Belgian-Prussian authority, went to Belgium, its forests a replacement for those destroyed by the German army in its 1918 retreat. The small industrial regions of Eupen and Malmédy (totalling 400 square miles) were also to go to Belgium, subject to their inhabitants' approval (Articles 33, 34), to support her industrial reconstruction. Northern Schleswig (seized from Denmark by Prussia and Austria in 1864, and then by Prussia alone in 1866) was to decide by plebiscite whether to return to Denmark (Article 109).

By far the greater and most contentious territorial losses Germany suffered were in the east. The major parts of Posen and West Prussia were to be ceded to the newly formed state of Poland, losing Germany approximately 18,000 square miles. Poland was to secure a land corridor to the sea carved from German territory. The fate of Upper Silesia (taken by Prussia from Austria in 1742) and parts of East and West Prussia were to be decided by plebiscite (Articles 88, 94), the concession secured by Lloyd George following German protests. The city port of Danzig (seized by Prussia from Poland in 1793), together with 750 square miles of hinterland, was to become a Free City under League of Nations protection and in customs union with Poland (Articles 100–104). The future of the port of Memel was to be decided by the Allies (Article 99). The amalgamation of Germany and Austria was forbidden without the unanimous concurrence of the Council of

the League of Nations (Article 80). As France had a permanent seat on the Council, this effectively denied the possibility
of such a union (the desire for which the new constitutions of
both Austria and Germany made clear). Germany recognised
the independence of Czechoslovakia and accepted the loss by
any of her nationals remaining in the area of their German
citizenship (Articles 81, 84).

Germany ceded her overseas colonies for assignment by the
League of Nations to their conquerors as mandates (Article
119). Germany's pre-war colonies had covered nine million
square miles of territory, with a population of 13 million.
When the spoils were shared out, Germany lost South-West
Africa to South Africa, East Africa to Britain, with a small
strip allocated to Belgium, and the port of Kionga to Portugal. France took the bulk of Togoland and the Cameroons,
a portion going to Britain. In the Pacific, islands north of
the Equator were mandated to Japan. German New Guinea,
Nauru and islands south of the Equator went to Britain,
German Samoa to New Zealand and remaining islands to
Australia.

All German rights in Shandong and Jiaozhou were ceded
to Japan, to the resentment of China, which refused to sign
the treaty. All Germany's pre-1914 trading concessions in
Egypt, Morocco, Liberia, Siam and China were terminated
and the Allies were to have concessions for five years on
certain imports into and exports from Germany. The rivers
Elbe, Oder, Niemen and Danube were internationalised and
the Kiel Canal opened to shipping of all nations (Articles
331, 380).

Germany accepted that she would be stripped of her military power. Conscription was ended and, the army was to be
reduced by April 1920 (later extended to January 1921) to

100,000 officers and men, each limited to a 12-year term of service. Germany was to have no more than seven infantry and three cavalry divisions. The General Staff was abolished (Articles 160, 173, 174). All armoured vehicles, tanks and military aircraft were forbidden, though not civilian aircraft (Article 198). Limitations were placed on the manufacture of weapons and ammunition and the import or export of war materials was forbidden (Article 170). The navy was limited to six battleships of 10,000 tons, six light cruisers, 12 destroyers and 12 torpedo boats. Submarines were outlawed and naval personnel were not to exceed 15,000 (Articles 181, 183). The east bank of the Rhine was to be permanently demilitarised to a depth of 32 miles (Articles 42, 43). All fortifications on the Baltic and North Sea coasts and on the island of Heligoland were to be demolished (Articles 115, 195).

ARTICLE 231 OF THE TREATY OF VERSAILLES

'The Allies and Associated Governments affirm and Germany accepts the responsibility of Germany and her allies for causing all the loss and damage to which the Allies and Associated Governments and their nationals have been subjected as a consequence of the war imposed upon them by the aggression of Germany and her allies.'

Germany agreed that the ex-Kaiser would be tried for offences against international morality and the sanctity of treaties. Holland – where Wilhelm had fled in November 1918 – would be asked to extradite him for trial before a special tribunal made up of five judges from Britain, the United States, France, Italy and Japan. In addition, other individuals were to be surrendered to the Allies for trial by court-martial for violating the laws and customs of war (Articles 227–230). Under Article 231 (the so-called 'war guilt' clause) Germany accepted her responsibility and that of her allies for the war, something she had already agreed in the November 1918 Armistice. The purpose of the clause was to provide a legal basis for the Allied claims for reparations that immediately followed on in the treaty. The Allies recognised that Germany did not have adequate resources to make complete reparation for all war damage. Germany was to make an initial payment of 20,000 million gold marks to meet the costs of the army of occupation and the provision of food and raw materials, subsequent amounts and payments to be determined by the Reparation Commission by 1 May 1921 (Articles 232–235).

In the meantime, Germany was to compensate the Allies for their shipping losses by surrendering all merchant vessels over 1,600 tons, half between 1,000 and 1,600 tons, a quarter of steam trawlers and a quarter of other fishing vessels. Germany was to build annually 200,000 tons of shipping for the Allies for five years. In addition, Germany agreed to deliver seven million tons of coal annually to France, eight million to Belgium and an equivalent amount to Italy for ten years to compensate for German destruction of mines. Germany was to pass specified numbers of cattle, horses, sheep and other livestock to Belgium and France in compensation for those stolen during the war (Annexes to Article 244). To ensure Germany fulfilled her obligations under the treaty, the Allies would occupy the left bank and bridgeheads of the Rhine for 15 years at German expense (Article 428). Inter-Allied Commissions of Control based in Germany would oversee fulfilment. Evacuation of the Rhineland would be gradual and in three five-yearly stages. Any subsequent violation of the demilitarisation of the area by Germany would be regarded as an act of war (Article 44). By signing the treaty Germany had accepted the Covenant of the League of Nations, while acknowledging that she was not, as yet, worthy of membership.

Scheidemann, who had resigned as Chancellor rather than take the burden of accepting the treaty, described the popular desperation of June 1919. 'The people were without clothing, underlinen, boots and shoes and – bread. The people must go on starving. "Sign! Then there'll be bread" – that was the hope of millions.'[7]

∞∞∞∞

The Hall of Mirrors at Versailles, where the treaty was to be signed, echoed with historical resonance for both France and Germany. It was in this chamber that Bismarck had proclaimed Wilhelm I German Emperor on 18 January 1871 following France's defeat by Prussia. It was also here that France had signed a humiliating armistice. At the subsequent Treaty of Frankfurt, France ceded Alsace-Lorraine to Germany and agreed to pay an indemnity over three years of five billion francs (twice what Prussia had spent fighting the war). France paid the imposition in two, anxious to rid herself of German occupying troops. For France the Hall of Mirrors had been the scene of shame; for Germany of triumph, the reward for military victory. The positions were now reversed. As if this were not symbolic enough, the day itself – 28 June – could hardly have been more significant. It was five years exactly since Gavrilo Princip had shot Archduke Franz Ferdinand in the streets of Sarajevo, setting off the train of events that culminated in war.

Müller and Bell left Friedrichstrasse station by ordinary train late on 26 June, arriving in Cologne the following morning. Here they waited a few hours for the special train that would take them across Belgium and France, accompanied by Allied officers. The train dragged painfully slowly across the devastated war zones, constantly halting at village stations or in mid-countryside. The delegates finally reached

Saint-Cyr-l'École, close to Versailles, at 2.50 a.m. on 28 June. After a few hours sleep at the Hôtel des Réservoirs, Müller and Bell went through the formalities of presenting their credentials at the Trianon Palace. The morning was cloudy, the sun breaking through about midday. Eleven regiments of French infantry and cavalry were moving into position to line the routes to the palace where the treaty would be signed. After lunch the delegates changed into morning coats and top hats, the formal wear demanded by diplomatic etiquette. At 2.45 p.m. four Allied colonels – British, French, American and Italian – presented themselves to the Germans as escorts for the 400-yard drive to the ceremony.

ooooo

The Allied delegates have already taken their places. At 2.10 p.m. the chief of protocol, a French foreign office official, places the leather-cased treaty on a small desk in the gleaming Hall of Mirrors, open and ready for signature. Clemenceau arrives shortly after two, carried in a flag-decked limousine between double lines of steel-blue helmeted infantrymen, bayonets fixed. The soldiers present arms. He is followed by Lloyd George and then by Wilson, who are both cheered by the watching crowd. Republican Guards stand on each step, sabres held at the salute. At 2.30 p.m. Clemenceau, who is to preside over the ceremony, walks into the Hall of Mirrors, stopping briefly to chat to a group of wounded and bemedalled French veterans. He takes his seat at a large horseshoe-shaped table in the middle of the room. Clemenceau sits almost exactly at the spot where Wilhelm I was proclaimed German Emperor 48 years before. Lloyd George and Wilson are among the last to enter the room, which overflows with distinguished guests – deputies, senators, generals – and members of the press. The American president and the British prime minister are seated either side of Clemenceau, the delegates from Germany's other wartime foes extending beyond them.

There is a hum of voices in the room. Clemenceau motions to the ushers to quieten the audience. The Republican Guards sheath their sabres. Clemenceau calls for the German delegation to be brought in. Müller and Bell have reached the palace shortly after 3 p.m. and are led by the chief of protocol through an anteroom busy with the wives of officers and politicians. They are barely noticed as they enter the Hall of Mirrors, taking their seats at seven minutes past three, Brazilians to their left, Japanese to their right. An acutely sensitive member of the British delegation records in his diary, 'The silence is terrifying ... They keep their eyes fixed away from those two thousand staring eyes, fixed upon the ceiling. They are deathly pale. They do not appear as representatives of a brutal militarism. The one [Bell] is thin and pink-eyelidded: the second fiddle in a Brunswick orchestra. The other [Müller] is moon-faced and suffering ... It is all most painful.' [8]

Clemenceau is as brusque as he had been in presenting the draft treaty to Brockdorff-Rantzau in May. He says the Allies and the German government have reached an agreement and signatures are now to be exchanged. 'They constitute an irrevocable undertaking to carry out loyally and faithfully and in their entirety all the terms of the Treaty.' [9] He calls the Germans forward to sign. In the course of his short speech, Clemenceau waves his hand in the direction of the table bearing the open treaty. Müller goes first, conscious of · an audience straining to gauge his demeanour and capture the instant. 'Nothing in my behaviour, walk, appearance, should be allowed in any way to betray us. I wanted our ex-enemies to see nothing of the deep pain of the German people, whose representative I was at this tragic moment.'[10] Müller puts his name to the treaty with a fountain pen at 3.12 p.m., followed quickly by Bell, using a pen he had taken from the hotel.

Relieved, the audience resumes the hubbub of conversation as Müller and Bell return to their places, the unpleasant duty almost concluded. Wilson rises to sign, smiling, shaking proffered hands as he makes his way to the desk. Lloyd George and the prime ministers of the British Dominions follow; then the French, the Italians, the Japanese. The smaller powers take their turn, gradually but swiftly filling the vellum pages of the treaty. Only China has refused to attend, angry at concessions made to Japan at her expense. At 3.50 p.m. Clemenceau declares the ceremony complete, the peace treaty an accomplished fact. He asks the delegates to remain until the Germans have left. As he ends his announcement French artillery begin to fire a salute outside the palace, the smoke and thunder of the guns mingling with the rising cheers of the crowd.

MÜLLER DESCRIBES THE INCIDENT OF THE FOUNTAIN PEN

'In Weimar I had already learnt from French newspapers that it was intended to have the Treaty signed with a special pen supplied by the "Leagues" to recover Alsace-Lorraine in France and the French Colonies. I had decided, even then, to avoid this deliberately prepared humiliation by signing with my own fountain pen. Dr Bell did not possess one, so in order to be on the safe side he secured a cheap pen from the hotel, rolled it in a piece of newspaper, and stuck it into his waistcoat pocket. He took it out as soon as we were called, and used it to set down his signature ... The Press all over the world scrupulously noted with many appropriate comments that I had used a fountain pen to sign a treaty. One Paris newspaper published a rather poor caricature with a malicious, but really witty, inscription: "Huns' last trick – Hermann Müller signs in invisible ink." That inspiration came too late.'[11]

ooooo

Müller and Bell left the Hall of Mirrors, escorted by the Allied officers who had accompanied them in less than an hour before. At the hotel Müller's rigid self-control evaporated. 'In the very second when I laid down my hat and coat in my room and was about to proceed to change my clothes a cold sweat such as I had never known in my life before broke out all over my body – a physical reaction which necessarily followed the unutterable psychic strain. And now, for the first time, I knew that the worst hour of my life lay behind me.'[12] The German delegates left Versailles at once, watching from their train the fireworks and rockets bursting over every village and town in celebration. Before leaving, the delegation issued a statement to the press, emphasising the German people's willingness to make every effort to comply with the treaty, but repeating their dissatisfaction with the conditions the Allies had imposed. 'We believe the Entente will, in their own interests, find it necessary to change some of the terms which they will come to see are impossible of execution ... Germany will make every effort to prove herself worthy of entry into the League of Nations.'[13]

The National Assembly ratified the treaty on 9 July by 208 votes to 115, a revealing number raising their hand against given that the vast majority of deputies had agreed only a fortnight before there was no alternative to signing. Ebert signed the ratification that evening, sending the document by courier to Versailles. As Germany digested what Müller and Bell had painfully accepted on her behalf, Allied foreign ministers and diplomats – the leading figures leaving once the major treaty had been signed – continued their work formally ending hostilities with their wartime enemies. The Treaty of

St Germaine-en-Laye was signed with Austria on 10 September, the Treaty of Neuilly with Bulgaria on 27 November, the Treaty of Trianon with Hungary on 4 June 1920, and, finally, the Treaty of Sèvres with Turkey on 10 August 1920.

ooooo

The Treaty of Versailles formally came into effect on 10 January 1920. But by that point the association of the three major Allied figures – Clemenceau, Wilson and Lloyd George – was fragmenting. Clemenceau, though pressed into compromises at the conference, continued to believe that the Allies' terms were just. However, many French disagreed, criticising him in particular for failing to secure France a defensive frontier on the Rhine. In January 1920 he stood for election by the Senate and Chamber of Deputies as president and was stunningly rejected. On 18 January he resigned as prime minister and went into political oblivion, where he remained until his death in 1929. In his memoirs, entitled *Grandeur and Misery of Victory*, Clemenceau warned that France would face another war with Germany, forecasting 1940 as the year of greatest danger. The leaders who succeeded Clemenceau sought a strict interpretation of the treaty and for its terms to be harshly enforced.

But it was Wilson, whose hopes for the Peace Conference had been greatest, who was to endure the bitterest political and personal disappointment. In September 1919 he collapsed while on a speaking tour trying to rouse support in the United States for what he had achieved in Europe. In October 1919 he suffered a stroke that left him incapacitated for months. Although awarded the Nobel Peace Prize for his work, he could not persuade Congress to ratify the treaty, the

Senate refusing on 19 November 1919 and again 19 March 1920 to vote the necessary two-thirds majority. The rejection of the treaty and the Covenant of the League of Nations prevented the United States from joining the League, which Wilson had made it his mission to create as the guarantor of world peace and the means by which Germany would be reconciled with the wartime Allies. Unable to run for re-election in 1920 because of his health, Wilson withdrew the United States from the Reparation Commission shortly before leaving office in March 1921. His successor as president, Warren Harding, agreed a separate peace with Germany in August.

By mid-1921, Lloyd George alone remained in office. He had revealed his misgivings concerning a punitive treaty in the Fontainebleau memorandum in March 1919 and again in his attempts in June to persuade Wilson and Clemenceau to meet some German objections. In December 1919 the economist John Maynard Keynes, who had attended the Peace Conference as a Treasury adviser but had resigned in despair, published *The Economic Consequences of the Peace*, castigating the way the treaty had been formulated and condemning above all the peacemakers' attitude towards reparations. The rising Labour Party, sister to Ebert's SPD, had condemned the treaty from the outset, arguing that its demands crippled the young democracy from birth, and demanded revision in its 1921 general election manifesto. Lloyd George, although savaged by Keynes, began increasingly to share that

'The real difficulty was not that the Treaty was exceptionally unfair but that the Germans thought it was, and in time persuaded others that it was.' [14]

SALLY MARKS, *THE ILLUSION OF PEACE. INTERNATIONAL RELATIONS IN EUROPE 1918–1933* outlook, but was only able to influence events until 1922, when he too lost office.

Germany had signed the treaty in June 1919 in the expectation that it would be subsequently revised, as Müller and Bell had said as their signatures dried. Although the compromises between Wilson, Clemenceau and Lloyd George had left many loose ends, the overall intention of the treaty had been to restrain rather than suppress Germany. This was not how most Germans saw it, smarting as they were from unexpected defeat. To them, Versailles was a *Diktat* rather than a compromise, a 'treaty of infamy'. The Allies had invited that response by refusing to involve Germany in formulating the terms, denying her politicians any sense that they shared responsibility for the treaty and encouraging the majority of Germans to consider themselves as victims.

Versailles has been seen as too harsh or too weak, one German historian writing, 'Too severe, since Germany could do no other, from the first moment onwards, than try to shake it off; too lenient, because Germany was not so far weakened as to be deprived of the hope and possibility of either extricating itself from the treaty or tearing it up.'[15] The objectives had been to ensure Germany would not present a significant military danger to Europe, to reconstruct war-damaged Belgium and France, and to guarantee stability for the new states in central and eastern Europe. Germany resented each of these objectives and would continue to press for revision until she was in a position to ignore the treaty's provisions. Germany presented the limits imposed on her armed forces by Versailles as a breach of trust on the part of the Allies. German governments would claim that the reductions had been accepted on the basis that all others powers would similarly reduce their armaments. Wilson had, however, written this into the Covenant of the League of Nations in a spirit of hope rather than expectation. The context of the limitation on Germany's ability to wage war was that the fact that Britain, France, Russia and Italy acting together had been unable to defeat Germany and victory had only been secured by the intervention of the United States.

There was much bitterness in Germany towards Article 231 of the treaty, which condemned her as responsible for the outbreak of war in 1914. Most, including Ebert, had seen their war as defensive. The Independent Socialists were prepared to accept 'war guilt' as a means of placing responsibility where it belonged, on the Imperial military and political elites rather than the German people. Bernstein, the father of 'revisionism', who had now returned to the SPD after two years as an Independent Socialist, said nine tenths of the Allied demands in the treaty were 'unavoidable necessities'. He urged the SPD to free itself from the burden it had imposed on itself by voting for war credits in August 1914. 'Only the truth, the whole truth, can help us.'[16] But the entire range of German political parties from the SPD to the far right denied Article 231's validity. For the SPD leadership this was because accepting Germany's sole responsibility would undermine the moral case for revision of the treaty. The problem with this position was that it opened the door for the nationalist right to denounce those responsible for signing the treaty as traitors to Germany, comrades of those who had inflicted the 'stab in the back' of November 1918.

Losses of German territory, including her colonies, were resented but to be expected. Alsace-Lorraine and northern Schleswig had been seized in the 19th century and were now being returned to their original owners. The transfer of two small industrial regions to Belgium and the guarantee of coal to France from the Saar were acknowledgements that these two states had suffered through war being fought on their soil. Germany had remained inviolate and unharmed from beginning to end. The overriding of the Wilsonian principle of national self-determination was more controversial. The new states of eastern and central Europe – most significantly Poland and Czechoslovakia – had risen from the ruins of the Austrian and Russian Empires. Their delegations presented themselves in Paris determined that their countries would survive politically and economically. Germany resented the resulting loss of territory, resources and population, arguing that national self-determination did not seem to apply in her case. The unlikelihood that Germany would ever be allowed to unite with Austria was further salt in the wound.

The final sense of resentment arose from reparations. The Germans could legitimately complain that they had been pressed to sign a 'blank cheque' at Versailles, agreeing to pay but having no idea how much until May 1921. Wilson had said in an address to the American people on 28 June 1919, 'It is a severe treaty in the duties and penalties it imposes upon Germany; but it is severe only because great wrongs done by Germany are to be righted and repaired; it imposes nothing that Germany cannot do; and she can regain her rightful standing in the world by the prompt and honorable fulfilment of its terms.'[17] But it was a military man, Marshal Foch, who declared as the treaty was being signed, 'This is not a peace. It is an armistice for 20 years.'[18] He echoed a joke circulating in Paris during the conference that the basis was being laid for a 'just and lasting war'.[19]

Last picture taken of Friedrich Ebert (14 days before his death on 28 February 1925)

The Legacy

The Reich President addresses the crowd after being sworn in at a ceremony in the National Theatre in Weimar, 21 August 1919

The Brittle Republic, 1919–25

When the National Assembly appointed Ebert provisional Reich President in February 1919, a reporter from the *Berliner Lokal-Anzeiger*, a nationalist daily, interviewed his wife. The family had only recently moved from the working-class Treptow neighbourhood to an imposing official residence attached to the Interior Ministry. The tone of the interview, which *The Times* reprinted, illustrated the snobbery Ebert, a man of lower-class origins not born to power, would face as Germany's first democratic head of state. The report described Frau Ebert as 'a typical workman's wife, without any servant, ready for any housework and accustomed to fetch even coals from the cellar'. The journalist noted that she had always made and mended the family's clothes, in a tone suggesting this was a matter for shame. 'Frau Ebert was quite prepared for malicious attacks upon her husband and herself,' he went on, 'but contemplates the prospect with indifference, as she is determined to retain her native pride of class.' Hugo Stinnes, a leading businessman with considerable influence over Ebert, invariably described him as 'the saddler'. Gustav Stresemann, the head of the conservative German People's

Party, complained in April 1919 that while the Kaiser had been the focus around which everything revolved, 'Ebert is no central point', a reflection as much on his personality as his origins.[1]

For all the driving ambition Ebert had shown during his career, his modesty and aversion to personal aggrandisement made a refreshing change (or a demeaning decline, depending on taste) from the Kaiser's imperious posturing. Reluctant to give non-political interviews or to be photographed outside his state duties, Ebert believed that the office, not the individual, was the object of esteem. The Reich President should act impartially, above party. This earned him the respect, if not the affection, of the liberal middle and working classes. But to the nationalist and monarchist right he was the illegitimate heir of the 1918 revolution, mythologised as the cause of Germany's defeat and the humiliation of Versailles. They shared a 'conviction that Germany was experiencing a decline in moral standards and a breakdown of social order'.[2] The radical left despised him as the betrayer of the proletariat, in thrall to the old regime. Even his own SPD, moderate as its members had acted in the revolutionary opportunity of November 1918, revealed a growing disappointment during his years in office, the saddlers' union expelling him and the party discussing the possibility of doing the same.

On 31 July 1919 the National Assembly adopted a republican constitution drafted by Hugo Preuss, a professor of constitutional law. The constitution was seen at the time as the most democratic in the world, with equal suffrage and an elaborate system of proportional representation. But the groups and forces that had been the pillars of Imperial Germany remained intact, their foundations hardly shaken by the revolution. Preuss was to suggest in 1925 that a discrepancy between the formally democratic constitution and the traditionally authoritarian civil service lay at the root of the Weimar Republic's weakness. Ebert ratified the document on 11 August and was inaugurated into office ten days later. As if foretelling the ill-fortune and ineptitude that would bedevil the Republic, Ebert's swearing-in ceremony had moments of embarrassing farce.

On the day of the inauguration, Germany's largest-circulation illustrated paper, the nationalist *Deutsche Tageszeitung*, printed a photograph of Ebert and Noske, now defence minister, wading in the Baltic Sea. Two heavily moustached, middle-aged men in bathing suits, pot-bellied, hands on hips, caught between surprise and embarrassment. Here, the illustration implied, is what has become of Germany, democracy displacing dignity. Ebert arrived at the National Theatre at 5 p.m., followed into the flower-decked hall by Chancellor Bauer and the cabinet, an organ playing solemnly. The seats set aside for the Independent Socialists and the German Nationalists were empty. A participant noted in his diary, 'When Ebert was supposed to take the oath, the text was nowhere to be found. A search ensued. An embarrassing interval as the organ ceased playing. Finally someone pushed his way through the frock coats with the page in hand.'[3]

After swearing his oath as Reich President, Ebert told the assembly: *This must remain to us if we desire to rebuild the Fatherland – deep love for the homeland and the tribe out of which each of us sprang, and to this must be joined sacred labour for the whole and the placing of one's self in the republic's service ... The essence of our Constitution shall above all be freedom, but freedom must have its law.* The ceremony complete, Ebert stepped to a balcony overlooking the square to address the crowd. *A people equal with equal rights – that is what this day shall signify to all Germans … Let us stand together in our people's hard struggle for life.*[4] The people cheered and a band played 'Deutschland über Alles'.

Within months the Republic was in peril, threatened by the institution in which Ebert had placed his trust in November 1918, the army. There had been hints of what was to come. In September 1919 the officer commanding troops in Berlin offered his opinion that the cabinet were a pack of rascals. Scheidemann said in a speech that he was surprised the government were taking so long to dismiss the general. Ebert called Scheidemann to his office, as furious as he had been when Scheidemann proclaimed the republic in November 1918. Scheidemann told him the general's sacking would have a salutary effect on all anti-Republican officers. Ebert reacted angrily. *I shall not think of doing so.*[5]

At the beginning of March the government ordered a Freikorps brigade quartered outside Berlin to disband in accordance with the Versailles treaty. On 10 March three generals, led by General Walter von Lüttwitz, the Freikorps founder, pressed Ebert to rescind the order, going on to demand Reichstag and presidential elections and a promise that the government would ignore the Versailles limitations on the army's size. Ebert refused and the government dismissed the general the next day. But on the night of 12/13 March, Lüttwitz marched the brigade into Berlin,

General Walter von Lüttwitz; founded the Freikorps

occupied government offices and proclaimed Wolfgang Kapp – a founding member of the annexationist Fatherland Party in 1917 and now co-leader with General Ludendorff of the Patriotic Association – chancellor. Kapp proposed to restore the monarchy. General Hans von Seeckt, head of the Truppenamt (which had replaced the General Staff) refused a command to disarm the rebels, telling defence minister Noske, 'When Reichswehr fires on Reichswehr, all comrade-

Wolfgang Kapp (1858–1922); founded the Deutsche Vaterlandspartei (German Fatherland Party) in 1917; after the failed putsch he was put in prison where he died awaiting trial.

ship between the officer corps has vanished.'[6] Ebert and the government fled, first to Dresden – where the local army commander doubted he could guarantee their safety – and then to Stuttgart.

Kapp Putsch in Berlin: proclamation of a new government on the Pariser Platz

Most army commanders and senior civil servants remained aloof, neither supporting nor opposing Kapp, waiting to see whether the Republic survived. But in Bavaria Reichswehr officers forced an SPD-led coalition to resign, replacing it with a right-wing state government. In Berlin, a general strike organised by the trade unions – Catholic as well as socialist – forced Kapp to abandon the rebellion and flee with Lüttwitz to Sweden on 17 March. Ebert was reluctant to acknowledge that his bargain with the army in November 1918 had come to nothing, that its commanders did not see their prime duty as the defence of the Republic. The generals – Seeckt, Groener and the retired Hindenburg – appealed for clemency for soldiers actively involved in the *putsch*. Ebert not only agreed, but went on to appoint Seeckt (who had disobeyed orders) head of the Reichswehr, rejecting demands from the trade unions for a purge of the army command, the senior bureaucracy and the judiciary.

But, as in January 1919, the army proved keen to go into action against the left, repressing a 'Red Army' of striking Socialists and Communists in the Ruhr and central Germany in March and April 1920, led by a general who had backed the Kapp conspirators only days before at the head of troops whose loyalty to the government had been ambiguous. Ebert subsequently exercised his authority as Reich President to issue a retrospective decree legalising the summary executions the army and Freikorps carried out against those who had defended the Weimar Republic against Kapp. He was always more sensitive to a threat from the left than the right, though the latter posed far greater dangers. It was as if Ebert felt compelled to prove that, as he had told Prince Max in 1918, he hated revolution *like sin*.

Ebert's friend Noske resigned as defence minister in the

wake of the *putsch*, along with Chancellor Bauer, Müller – one of the German signatories at Versailles and Ebert's oldest party friend – briefly taking the post until elections in June. Writing to a Swedish socialist on 16 April, Ebert blamed the failure to create an effective German democracy on the Versailles Treaty. German voters expressed their repugnance to Versailles in the June elections, punishing the 'Weimar coalition' they held responsible. Compared with February 1919, the SPD share of the vote fell from 37.9 per cent to 21.7 per cent, the Centre from 16.7 per cent to 13.6 per cent and the Democrats from 18.5 per cent to 8.5 per cent. Overall the coalition share plummeted from 78 per cent to 44.6 per cent. The Independents, to the left of the SPD, increased their popular vote from 10.3 per cent to 17.9 per cent, but the real gains were on the right. The People's Party share rose to 13.9 per cent and the German Nationalists to 15.1 per cent, and the two parties went on to form a minority coalition with the Centre under Konstantin Fehrenbach. The SPD's withdrawal from government signified the collapse of Ebert's dream of a reforming parliament democracy and Germany's hope of a stable democratic future. It was only a slight exaggeration to say that Germany had become 'a Republic without republicans'.

ooooo

On 18 January 1921 Ebert issued a proclamation celebrating the 50th anniversary of the establishment of the German Empire. It would have been impossible to avoid any reference to Versailles on an occasion of emotional significance to all Germans, whatever their politics. Ebert said that in spite of all Germany remained a unified state. *Even if, today, we*

have to look with sorrow towards our German compatriots
who against their will have been separated from the lands of
their kindred, and towards sorely-tried Austria, who long-
ingly stretches out her arms to us, as we to her, we must be
determined to maintain our domestic unity.[7]

The League of Nations took over administration of the
Saar, to which France had been given sole access to coal for
15 years under the treaty, on 26
February 1920. While only a
temporary loss, some Germans
feared it might be the prelude
to a permanent seizure. On 20
September 1920 Germany ceded
Eupen and Malmédy to Belgium.
The 1910 census had shown the
populations to be 83 per cent German-speaking, 13 per cent
Walloon, and there was bitterness over the pressures placed
on the German population to accept their fate. Changes in the
north were less contentious. In February and March 1920 the
population of the German province of North Schleswig voted
75 per cent in a plebiscite held in the northern part to revert to
Denmark, 75 per cent in the southern part to remain German,
and these expressions of preference were honoured.

The settlement on Germany's eastern frontiers was more
fraught. On 11 February 1920 the League of Nations took
over formal administration of Danzig and its hinterland from
Germany. As the terms of the treaty had demanded, Poland
absorbed West Prussia in January 1920, giving the new state
a corridor to the Baltic (and almost 400,000 Germans), but in
plebiscites in July the district of Marienwerder voted to remain
German, as did most of the Allenstein area of East Prussia.
Events in Upper Silesia were dramatic. In February 1920 Allied

> **We have to look with sorrow towards our German compatriots who against their will have been separated from the lands of their kindred.**
>
> EBERT, 18 JANUARY 1921

troops, predominantly French, were deployed to end clashes between Germans and Poles. Polish forces made a further attempt in August to evict the German Freikorps. On 21 March 1921 Upper Silesia voted 60 per cent to remain German, 40 per cent to become Polish. Most Germans believed this meant they would retain the entire area. In May Polish forces routed Freikorps troops, taking control of two-thirds of the region before the Allies forced a cease-fire. The Reichswehr commander, General von Seeckt, was prepared to push the Poles back but Ebert restrained him, anxious not to antagonise the French and British in the midst of reparations negotiations.

On 20 October 1921 the Allied Supreme Council, acting on a League of Nations recommendation, partitioned Upper Silesia, the rich mining and industrial area in the east (where 44 per cent of the inhabitants had voted to remain German) going to Poland, Germany retaining the less-prized west. This contradicted the results of the March 1921 plebiscite, but on 15 May 1922 Germany agreed the division and the loss of over a million citizens by convention with Poland. The new state of Czechoslovakia contained almost four million German speakers in the Sudetenland, remnants of the collapsed Austro-Hungarian Empire. Memel, again containing a predominantly German population, was also lost. The area had been under Allied administration since February 1920. On 10 January 1923 troops from the newly independent Lithuania marched into Memel, forcing the mainly French garrison to withdraw, absorbing the territory despite Allied protests.

Versailles had deprived Germany of her colonies in Africa and the Pacific. Johannes Bell was colonial minister when he was persuaded to be a signatory to the treaty. Within weeks he told the German Colonial Society that the government would demand that Germany be readmitted into the ranks of the colonial powers. 'Rather than sit back with arms folded, we must now work unflinchingly to ensure that when the inevitable revision of the Versailles treaty occurs Germany will have her colonial rights restored.'[8] Although the Colonial Society kept the issue alive through the 1920s, the return of the colonies was not pressed until the Nazis became entrenched in power in the 1930s.

There was also the matter of the 'war criminals'. The treaty had demanded that the former Kaiser face trial for offences against international morality with other Germans accused of violating the laws and customs of war. On 15 January 1920, a few days after the Versailles treaty came into force, the Allies asked the government of the Netherlands – where Wilhelm had fled in November 1918 – to extradite him. The Dutch refused, somewhat to the relief of the Allied governments, the immediate post-war thirst for personal revenge having waned. The Allies also submitted to the German government the names of 900 individuals they wished to press charges against. These included Crown Prince Wilhelm, the military commanders Hindenburg and Ludendorff, and Bethmann-Hollweg, who had been Imperial Chancellor on the outbreak of war in 1914. The German government refused, fearing a destabilising public anger if it acquiesced in the demand for generals – who had led the army in what the country believed to have been a defensive war – to face trial abroad.

In February 1920 the Allies reduced their demands, proposing to bring a few minor figures before a German court in Leipzig. The cases were presented from May to July 1920. Of the six individuals accused by the British – three prisoner-of-war camp commandants and three submarine commanders – five were convicted. France tabled charges against five individuals, of whom one was convicted, and Belgium one, who was acquitted. The matter was then dropped and no more was heard at an official level of what had now become an embarrassing charade.

Inextricably linked with accusations of war crimes was the question of 'war guilt', which Germany had been forced to acknowledge under Article 231 of the treaty. As early as June 1919 the German Foreign Office had been selecting and disseminating material from its archives to present German actions in the build up to the war in their best light. In January 1921, as the reparations issue was coming to a head, the foreign and finance ministries allocated a million marks to establish a pseudo-scholarly Centre for the Study of the Causes of the War, with a further 200,000 marks for German missions abroad to publicise the results. One hostile study has no doubt that this 'pollution of American, British, and French historical understanding of the origins of the Great War must have helped to undermine faith in the need to maintain the irenic clauses of the 1919 treaty'. By creating a 'national alibi', Weimar governments sought to construct a rallying point to unite the entire political spectrum in a single patriotic cause, while at the same time laying the ground for a revision of Versailles.[9] If 'war guilt' were disproved, the reasoning went, the liabilities imposed on Germany would be shown to have no validity.

ooooo

The early 1920s saw the beginning of a cat-and-mouse game over reparations that would last until their final abandonment in 1932. The victors at Versailles had intended Article 231 to serve as the legal basis for their demands, though the calculation of the amount was delayed until 1921. In the meantime, Germany was to make an interim payment of 20,000 million gold marks in cash and kind (mainly coal and timber). By 1921 Germany had paid only 5,000 million of this. In January 1921 a conference of Allied ministers in Paris set the final amount of reparations at 226,000 million gold marks, to be paid annually from 1 May 1921, with a final payment on 1 May 1963. In addition, Germany was to pay an annual sum equivalent to the value of 12 per cent of her exports. Germany was given four days to accept or present counter-proposals.

In the midst of these negotiations, with Germany arguing her economy was too fragile to meet Allied demands, Ebert was embarrassed by reports in the foreign press of the unduly luxurious life in Berlin, with expensively-dressed revellers crowding the city's restaurants and night-clubs. He wrote to the vice chancellor asking him to curb what he called *the dissolute pursuit of pleasure becoming manifest at a time when the country is plunged in misery*. Warming to his high-minded theme, Ebert went on, *Individual dignity and the dignity of Germany demand that each man who feels himself bound up with the destiny of his people should abstain more than ever from noisy pursuit of pleasure.*[10]

When the Foreign Minister, Walther Rathenau, gave Germany's response to the Allies, there was anger – from the French particularly – at its arrogance. He demanded that the payment linked to Germany's exports should be dropped and the overall total reduced to 30,000 million marks, less than a seventh of what the Allies had proposed. Further, payment would be conditional on an early withdrawal of the Allied occupation forces and Germany's right to retain the whole of Upper Silesia. On 8 March French troops marched into

Düsseldorf, Duisburg and Ruhrort, threatening to seize the entire industrial heartland of the Ruhr. Ebert complained that the Allies were acting entirely unreasonably. *Not only we ourselves, but also our children and grandchildren are to become working slaves of our opponents ... Our opponents have openly broken the Peace Treaty of Versailles and have proceeded to occupy further stretches of German territory. We cannot oppose force to force.*

> Not only we ourselves, but also our children and grandchildren are to become working slaves of our opponents.
>
> **EBERT, 8 MARCH 1921**

We are defenceless. We can, however, proclaim it far and wide so that it shall be heard by all who still recognise the voice of righteousness.[11]

When the Reparation Commission sent a final and significantly reduced demand in May, the Fehrenbach cabinet resigned. The overall payment was now to be 132,000 million gold marks, the bulk to be paid by Germany, the remainder by her wartime allies. Joseph Wirth formed a new government and the Reichstag voted to agree to the demand. Germany paid the first instalment of 1,000 million marks at the end of August, borrowing from London banks to do so, and then requested a moratorium on further cash payments. The wearing down process appeared to be working and at a conference in Cannes in January 1922 the Reparation Commission temporarily relieved Germany of cash payments and reduced the quotas for coal and timber deliveries. Lloyd George sought to go further at a conference in Genoa in April, hoping to draw both Germany and the Soviet Union into the European concert and revive trade. His hopes foundered when Germany signed a treaty with the Soviets at Rapallo on 16 April, re-establishing diplomatic and economic relations and absolving one another of reparations. The German ambassador to the Soviet Union was Brockdorff-Rantzau, who had rejected the Versailles treaty in May 1919.

A by-product of Rapallo was the help it gave Germany in further evading the military conditions imposed at Versailles. The Rapallo Treaty contained no secret military clauses as some Allied politicians suspected; none were necessary as there had been active military co-operation between Germany and the Soviet Union since 1920. Officers of the Reichswehr and the Red Army co-operated in training and in rebuilding both states' arms industries. General von Seeckt, whom Ebert appointed Reichswehr commander in 1920 after he had refused to act against the Kapp Putsch, envisaged joint action with the Soviets to destroy Poland and restore Germany's eastern borders. After Rapallo, Germany constructed weapons, aircraft and tank factories in Russia, taking advantage of the country's isolation to train troops. Despite Seeckt's aversion to political control of the army, Ebert was presumably aware of this systematic evasion of Versailles. Lord d'Abernon, the British ambassador to Germany, noted in his diary in November 1923, 'Von Seeckt is an intimate with Ebert, the two being close friends.' [12]

The jousting over reparations continued through 1922, Germany seeking a moratorium on payments, Clemenceau's successor Raymond Poincaré demanding the seizure of the Ruhr and the left bank of the Rhine as security. As an already damaging inflation worsened, Germany could not afford to buy gold to pay reparations in cash. On 22 November Wirth resigned, to be replaced as chancellor by a non-party businessman, Wilhelm Cuno. Ebert was angry at the SPD's refusal to enter Cuno's government, while party members accused Ebert of putting big business in power. At the end of December the

Reparation Commission charged Germany with defaulting on timber and coal deliveries. With a Franco-Belgian occupation of the Ruhr imminent, Ebert accused the Allies of threatening the core of German economic life, industry and the working class. He said Germany had expected peace at Versailles; instead she had received injustice. *Against these acts of force we protest before Europe and the whole world … Behave with dignity in the presence of foreign wielders of power until the morning dawns which gives the right that is due you and your freedom.*[13]

On 11 January 1923 60,000 French and Belgian troops accompanied engineers into the Ruhr to secure coal Germany had failed to deliver. Ebert had prepared a campaign of passive resistance with business, SPD and trade union leaders, convening a meeting on 8 January and presiding over a cabinet session the following day. For perhaps the first time since 1918, he stood at the head of a united Germany as workers, employers and state officials mounted a general strike in the Ruhr, refusing all co-operation with the occupiers. The cost to the national treasury was immense, printing presses in Berlin rather than taxation providing the cash needed for food and wage subsidies, intensifying Germany's already vertiginous inflation. But by late summer the resistance had proved hopeless. France and Belgian, rather than withdrawing their armies, had strengthened them. Poincaré refused to negotiate unless Germany backed down.

On 12 August Cuno resigned. Stresemann of the People's Party formed a 'grand coalition' including the SPD, and issued a joint decree with Ebert ending the strikes in the Ruhr. Germany renewed reparation payments in kind in September. Stresemann had taken a step that promised to end the logjam in Germany's post-war international relations, returning to a policy of 'fulfilment'. In October his government asked the Reparation Commission to reconsider the burden imposed on Germany and to examine her economic position.

Germany's position was indeed calamitous as hyperinflation raged from mid-1922 into 1923. In 1914 four marks had bought one US dollar. By January 1923 there were 17,972 marks to the dollar, by August a million, and in November 4,200,000 million. The Empire had bequeathed a massive national debt to the Republic, rising from 5,000 million marks in 1913 to 144,000 million in 1919. The Imperial government had financed the war largely through loans rather than taxation and the Republic continued this practice to meet increased health, education and welfare spending. Republican governments were reluctant to raise taxes, for fear of being accused by German nationalists that this was necessary to meet the demands of Versailles. But a further advantage was that the unstable currency created difficulties for the Allies in calculating Germany's liabilities for reparations. By late 1922 the national debt had risen to 469,000 million marks.

German opinion blamed hyperinflation on an unfavourable trade balance, which in turn was blamed on reparations and therefore on Versailles. The Allies pointed to the country's budget deficit and excessive use of the printing press, accusing the government of using inflation to evade Germany's liabilities. The Allies pressed the government to balance the national budget through taxation. By the summer of 1923, as passive resistance in the Ruhr continued, 300 mills were devoted solely to supplying paper to 150 printing firms running 2,000 presses to turn out banknotes. Big business benefited, with debts wiped out almost overnight and tax bills falling in value between demand and payment. By October 1923 only 1 per cent of government income came through taxation, the remainder from printing. Living standards fell for the workers, the lower middle class and the professions, as wages – sometimes paid three times a day and spent immediately – never caught up with rising prices. Non-unionised workers – clerks, farm labourers, domestic servants – fared worst of all, pensioners and the middle class on fixed incomes hardly better.

In October the newly-established Rentenbank issued a Rentenmark with a value equivalent to the pre-war gold mark or a trillion Reichsmarks. The new currency was nominally exchangeable for bonds underwritten by land and industrial plant. Stability returned as the Rentenmark held its value. But a legacy of bitterness remained, in the psychologically-scarred middle class most of all. Confidence in the Republic, and by extension in parliamentary democracy, was shattered only four years into its life.

ooooo

The summer and autumn of 1923 marked the high point of armed threats against the Republic's stability, with action from both left and right, and mounting separatist sentiment in the Rhineland encouraged by France and Belgium. Secret right-wing movements had been growing in strength since the early 1920s, notably Organisation Consul, an offshoot of the Freikorps. In August 1921 two Consul members assassinated Erzberger, the leading Centre Party politician who had negotiated the 1918 armistice. Rathenau was the next major victim. Both were connected with Versailles – Erzberger had recommended acceptance, Rathenau worked for 'fulfilment'. There is no doubt that Ebert was also on Consul's death list. Following the murders the Reichstag passed a Law for the Protection of the Republic to counter the activities of extremist organisations. Bavaria refused to recognise the legislation. In August 1923 Ebert issued a decree, countersigned by the Cuno cabinet, extending the Reich government's powers to suppress extremist activity.

In Saxony and Thuringia Communists had entered coalition governments with the Socialists while at the same time preparing for a rising. On 26 September Ebert and Stresemann, who had replaced Cuno as chancellor, proclaimed a state of emergency throughout Germany, passing temporary executive power to local military commanders. At the end of October Reichswehr troops entered Saxony following the state chancellor's refusal to disband the armed Communist units, replacing him with a People's Party commissar. The government seemed less willing to take decisive action against the nationalist right in Bavaria. Local radical right-wingers had booed and spat on Ebert when he visited Munich in 1922, denouncing him as a traitor.

In the continuing political crisis following the abandonment of passive resistance in the Ruhr, the Bavarian state government appointed the nationalist Gustav von Kahr as commissar with dictatorial powers. In October the local military commander, General Otto von Lossow, ignored Stresemann's instruction to assert the Republic's authority. Ebert's friends in the SPD urged him to make himself dictator to crush the right. He refused, replying, *First, all parliamentary methods must be exhausted*.[14] On 3 November Ebert decided the time had come to enforce the government's will with troops. Seeckt, the army commander, repeated what he had said in March 1920, that Reichswehr did not fire on Reichswehr.

Seeckt did, however, warn Kahr and Lossow not to involve themselves in nationalist intrigue against the Republic. On 8 November Adolf Hitler – who had led the National Socialist

German Workers' Party since 1921 – burst into a rally Kahr was holding in the Bürgerbräukeller in Munich, the Bavarian capital, with a band of armed stormtroopers. Believing the Republic to be on the point of collapse, he announced the overthrow of the Bavarian and Reich governments, forcing Kahr to declare a provisional regime headed by Hitler, Lossow and Ludendorff. The following morning Hitler and Ludendorff led a march into the city centre, where police – not the Reichswehr – halted them. Fourteen of the marchers and three police were killed in the shooting that followed and Hitler's bid for power collapsed. In a subsequent trial, he was sentenced to five years' imprisonment, of which he served only nine months.

Angered by what they saw as Stresemann's and Ebert's willingness to act more softly against the right than the left, the SPD withdrew from the coalition government on 23 November. Ebert was incensed, telling the party's executive committee, *What you have done to precipitate the fall of the chancellor will be forgotten in six weeks, but you will experience the consequences of your stupidity for another ten years.*[15]

> **The war broke off our international commerce abruptly, whilst the dictated peace has cruelly crippled it.**
> **EBERT, 11 MAY 1924**

The turmoil of 1923 – the occupation of the Ruhr, hyperinflation and threats from right and left – over, the Republic seemed on the brink of a secure future. On 13 February 1924 Ebert ended the state of emergency. Even the reparations issue appeared close to settlement. On 21 January an American banker, Charles Dawes, had met representatives of the British, Belgian, French, Italian and German governments in Paris to begin discussions on restructuring payments. Ebert made his first visit to the Rhineland, still occupied by Allied troops, and complained at a trade fair about the continuing impact of Versailles. *The war broke off our international commerce abruptly, whilst the dictated peace has cruelly crippled it.*[16]

Dawes' report to the Reparation Commission in April reduced the burden significantly. Ebert was determined the Reichstag should accept the terms, warning that he would use his powers to dissolve the legislature if members refused to co-operate. Germany would make no payments for two years. Then she would pay 1,000 million gold marks in the first year, rising to 2,500 million in the fifth and subsequent years, together with an additional percentage dependent on the country's prosperity. Germany's finances would be reorganised under international supervision and the Allies were to oversee parts of the state's assets, mainly the railways. France and Belgium were to withdraw from the Ruhr (as they did finally in August 1925) and Germany was guaranteed an international loan of 800 million marks. One writer says tellingly: 'From the start Germany viewed the plan as a temporary expedient to remove the French from the Ruhr and keep reparations minimal. Revision as soon as payments became onerous was taken for granted in Germany.'[17]

Dawes ushered in a period of prosperity for Germany, though the trauma of hyperinflation haunted the middle class. States, local authorities and industry took advantage of loans, mainly American, to construct new schools, public housing, hospitals and factories. A new era in Germany's international relations also appeared to beckon. In September Ebert chaired a cabinet meeting that agreed to seek speedy entry to the League of Nations, the only forum at which questions of disarmament, the administration of the Saar and the protection of German minorities could be settled. But for Ebert personally, the outlook was less cheerful. In

1924 the saddlers' union, which he had joined in 1889, expelled him. A motion put at the SPD conference that year to do the same was defeated but nonetheless pained Ebert. Chief among the union and party rank-and-file's grievances was Ebert having signed a decree underwriting employers' demands for an end to the eight-hour day, a valued achievement of the 1918 revolution.

Charles Dawes

The next, and final, attack on Ebert came from the right. In early 1924 the editor of the *Mitteldeutsche Zeitung* published a letter from a Bavarian nationalist accusing Ebert of treason for his part in the January 1918 munitions workers' strike. He challenged Ebert to disprove the charge in court. Ebert had confronted similar accusations and had been exonerated in each case. On 9 December Ebert, having accepted the challenge, said in a statement read to the court he had been against the January action and had joined the strike committee solely to bring it to an early end. Scheidemann gave evidence on 12 December that he and Ebert had been criticised on the committee as 'strike stranglers'. On 14 December Ebert's lawyer read from a letter Hindenburg had written in December 1918 declaring Ebert 'a true German patriot'. The verdict on 23 December came as a blow to Ebert. The judge agreed the editor was guilty of a technical libel but said Ebert had committed treason in supporting the strike, whatever his reasons.

Ebert was ill during the course of the trial but refused treatment for fear it would be seen as a plea for sympathy. On 23 February 1925 he was taken to hospital in Charlottenburg where he underwent surgery for appendicitis. At first

Ebert's funeral cortège passing the Brandenburg Gate in Berlin

he seemed to be recovering but two days later his condition worsened. On 28 February at 10.15 a.m. Ebert died in his sleep, his wife and family at the bedside. His body first lay in the hospital room, the bed decked with flowers by the sisters of the St Vincent de Paul Catholic order. On 1 March a hearse took the coffin to his office to lie in state, draped with the black-red-gold flag of the Republic. A copy of the Weimar Constitution lay on the desk where Ebert had left it, his horn-rimmed spectacles holding the page open. After a funeral ceremony at the Reichstag, Ebert's body was carried by train for burial in Heidelberg on 5 March.

When the government placed a bill before the Reichstag for the state to meet the costs of Ebert's funeral, the Communists and Nazis voted against, the left calling him a traitor to the working class, the right a traitor to the nation. It was a Nazi, Josef Goebbels, who in 1933 came close to summing up the tragedy of Ebert's political life. 'We will make no compromises. The Marxists made compromises and see what happened to them.'[18] Ebert had aspired to no more than a liberal democracy, but to achieve it he had compromised with the most reactionary sections of German society, the generals above all, and in doing so had undermined the democracy he sought.

7

The Unravelling of Versailles, 1925–45

With Ebert's death and Hindenburg's election as his successor as Reich President in April 1925, Germany gave the impression of having turned full circle in seven years. Stresemann, foreign minister from 1923–9, commented privately that the German people had shown they did not want a president but 'a man in uniform ... with a lot of medals'.[1] Hindenburg was an early proponent of the 'stab in the back' legend that Germany's ills arose from the socialist-liberal treachery of 1918. But it had been Hindenburg who had pleaded for an armistice, who had told Ebert (via Groener) that the army command would support the new republican government, and who had made it clear there was no choice but to sign the Treaty of Versailles.

Hindenburg remained an authoritarian and a monarchist – there were rumours, not true, that he had sought the ex-Kaiser's permission before allowing his name to go forward as a candidate – but he proved a disappointment to those on the right who hoped his presidency would see a more aggressive stance towards Britain and France over Versailles. Stresemann

Final session of the Locarno Treaty conference in London
1. Schubert, 2. Stresemann, 3. Luther, 4. Scialoja, 5. Baldwin, 6. A. Chamberlain,
7. Briand, 8. Berthelot, 9. Skrzczynski, 10. Vandervelde

followed a conciliatory policy in which 'fulfilment' of Versailles in the short term laid the ground for substantial revision in the long term. Hindenburg, to the annoyance of the German Nationalists, backed Stresemann over two crucial developments, the Treaty of Locarno and the Young Plan on reparations.

The ground for the Locarno Treaty was prepared by the British Labour prime minister Ramsay MacDonald, a friend of Ebert's, who believed that the weakness of German democracy lay in the treatment the Allies had meted out since Versailles in 1919, which he considered had fuelled the forces of nationalism. The Labour Party had consistently opposed the demand for reparations. Austen Chamberlain, the British foreign secretary closely involved in bringing the treaty to fruition, described the agreement at Locarno as a 'noble work of appeasement'. Stresemann's guiding principle was that removing the French threat – a repetition of the 1923 Ruhr occupation – required easing France's mind about any future danger Germany might pose to her. Secure in the west, Germany would have a free hand in the east.

Under the treaty, signed in October 1925, Germany, France and Belgium renounced the use of force to make frontier changes in the west, underwritten by Britain and Italy. Germany accepted the western borders imposed at Versailles, including the loss of Alsace-Lorraine, while France effectively abandoned any hopes of annexing the Rhineland, which Germany agreed would remain demilitarised. (Following Locarno Allied occupation troops evacuated the first zone of the Rhineland in February 1926 and the second zone in November 1929.) Stresemann was acknowledging the facts on the ground that had followed Germany's defeat in 1918, while contriving to make this appear a concession, a balancing act that angered right-wing parties at home. Germany maintained her intention to alter the eastern frontiers imposed in 1919–20, but assured Poland and Czechoslovakia she would not do so forcibly. Versailles ensured that, for the moment at least, Germany was in no position to achieve any of her ambitions on the battlefield. Germany was also promised admission to the League of Nations, with a permanent seat on the Council, which she took up in September 1926. In an atmosphere of hope that European security had been guaranteed, the French foreign minister Aristide Briand and Stresemann were jointly awarded the Nobel Peace Prize in 1926.

The second major development for Germany in the late 1920s was the Young Plan. Germany continued to complain that meeting reparations payments under the Dawes Plan, largely through American loans, was unsettling her economy. In 1929 the League of Nations appointed a committee of financial experts under the American banker Owen Young to re-examine the issue. Young reported on 7 June 1929. The original demand made by the Reparations Commission in April 1921 had been 132,000 million gold marks. Young now set the total German payment at 37,000 million gold marks, payable annually over 59 years on a sliding scale. Instalments would be postponed if Germany could prove hardship. Controls by the Allies and the United States over German state finances imposed by Dawes were to be removed and Germany would receive a loan of 1,200 million marks.

Germany accepted the Young Plan, a substantially better deal than Dawes, but added a demand for the evacuation of the remainder of the Rhineland and the return of the Saar, which was under League of Nations administration. France refused to contemplate handing back the Saar and said there would be no Rhineland evacuation until Germany showed signs of making a payment. Britain accepted the French position on the Saar but threatened a unilateral withdrawal from the Rhineland. In August 1929 the loose ends were tied up at a 'Conference for the Final Liquidation of the War' at The Hague. On 30 June 1930 the last Allied troops left the Rhineland, almost five years before the date set at Versailles. As one historian comments, Germany was now 'paying less than half of what she would have owed under the Dawes Plan. For this reduction, her reward was the Rhineland.'[2]

Advantageous as it appeared, the Young Plan provoked a surge of nationalist agitation in Germany. The right did not want reparations modified; they wanted them abandoned. In July 1929 Alfred Hugenberg, the leader of the German Nationalists, formed a committee to press the government to reject the proposals. He invited Hitler, whose Nazi Party was gaining strength on the right, to join the campaign. The committee was able to force a plebiscite on a 'Law against the Enslavement of the German People' on 22 December, rejecting both the Young Plan and the 'war guilt lie'. The Nationalist-Nazi campaign won the support of a little under 14 per cent of the electorate, 5.8 million voters. In the event, Germany had made few of the payments Young required before the Depression took hold in 1931.

In June 1931 the US President Herbert Hoover proposed a year's moratorium on reparations payments and the repayment of debts owed by Britain and France. When the moratorium expired, a conference at Lausanne in July 1932 relieved Germany of all reparations obligations with a final payment of 3,000 million gold marks when she was able, subject to the Allies reaching agreement with the United States on their wartime debts. An agreement was never reached and Germany made no further reparation payment. Estimates of what Germany paid overall vary, but what is clear is that by 1931 it was hardly more than the 2,000 million gold marks payment she had agreed at Versailles to make by 1 May 1921 and that much of what Germany did pay in cash had been based on loans from the United States, Britain and France.

ooooo

With the final collapse of the Weimar Republic under the pressure of the world financial crisis of the early 1930s, and the coming to power of the Nazis under Hitler in January 1933, the final unravelling of Versailles began. Successive German governments had blamed the treaty for the weakness of democracy, though the irony was that condemnation of Versailles was shared by the political right, centre and left. The distinction was that the right blamed the left for Versailles to avoid acknowledging that Germany had been led to defeat by a nationalist regime. The democratic left and centre believed that Versailles, particularly the war guilt clause and reparations, had handicapped the Republic from birth, and sought a path through fulfilment to revision. The nationalist right saw fulfilment as a surrender that followed inevitably from the 'stab in the back' of 1918 and agitated against the Republic on that basis. Their agitation culminated in the arrival of Hitler as chancellor.

ADOLF HITLER'S CULPRITS
'The themes of his speeches varied little: the contrast of Germany's strength in a glorious past with its current weakness and national humiliation – a sick state in the hands of traitors and cowards who had betrayed the Fatherland to its powerful enemies; the reasons for the collapse in a lost war unleashed by these enemies, and behind them, the Jews; betrayal and revolution brought about by criminals and Jews; English and French intentions of destroying Germany, as shown in the Treaty of Versailles – the "Peace of Shame", the instrument of Germany's slavery ...'[3]

Ian Kershaw, *Hitler 1889–1936: Hubris*

Hitler's political propaganda on his journey to power had centred on the national humiliation of Versailles, the war guilt clause, reparations and the loss of German territory and population. The new government observed the anniversary of the signing of the treaty on 28 June 1933 as a day of mourning and protest, with flags at half-mast on official buildings and a rally in Berlin addressed by Nazi leaders. *Der Tag* reported, 'It is widely pointed out that the struggle for revision and equality has a much better prospect of success now after the National Revolution and under the leadership of Hitler.'[4] Whether or not Hitler had a specific 'programme' for German domination of Europe, the demolition of what he considered the shackles of Versailles proceeded step by step from 1935 until the invasion of Poland in 1939. The return of the Saar to Germany following a plebiscite on 13 January 1935 was in accord with the Treaty of Versailles. Over 90 per cent of the area's half-million population voted to place themselves under Nazi control, including the majority of former Social Democrat and Communist supporters. Any further territorial alterations would require the threat, if not the use, of force.

Article 160 of the Versailles Treaty limited Germany's army to 100,000 volunteers, devoted exclusively to maintaining internal order and securing the frontiers. But the objective of the army command throughout the 1920s had been to rebuild the armed forces and restore Germany as a great power. Rearmament was a necessary precondition for overthrowing Versailles, enabling Germany to gain through force, or the threat of force, what Britain and France would not give through negotiation. Although the army flagrantly evaded the restrictions imposed at Versailles from 1920 onwards, the Reichswehr's capacity remained at a level that posed no threat to Germany's neighbours. The situation was to be transformed under the Nazi government, with an expansion in the army and navy and the establishment of an air force, which had specifically been banned at Versailles.

Wilson had intended general disarmament to be a means of creating security, but without security no European power was prepared to disarm, leading to the not unjustified complaint by Germany that only she was expected to adhere to the League of Nations Covenant. In September 1932 Germany walked out of the disarmament conference at Geneva, returning in December only when Britain and France proposed allowing a doubling of Reichswehr strength to 200,000. But in April 1933 Hitler told his cabinet that conferences were no place to resolve

Germany's urgent need to rearm. On 14 October Germany gave notice that she was withdrawing permanently from the disarmament conference and the League of Nations.

When the French National Assembly approved an extension of conscription from one to two years on 15 March 1935, Hitler informed the British, French and Italian ambassadors to Berlin the following day that Germany would be introducing military conscription and embarking on a major rearmament programme, with an army of 36 divisions, half a million men, armoured divisions, a stronger navy and an air force. Special editions of German newspapers praised this decisive blow against Versailles. At a military parade in Berlin on 17 March, defence minister General Werner von Blomberg, declared that Germany 'would never again capitulate and never put its signature to treaties which injured its honour, its security, or its vital rights.'[5]

The Allies – Britain, France and Italy – formally protested and at a meeting in Stresa on 11 April pledged to uphold the Locarno Pact, which had guaranteed Germany's western borders, and Austria's integrity. But Britain undermined this firm position by signing a naval agreement with Germany in June accepting the construction of a fleet 35 per cent the size of her own and a submarine force of equal strength. Britain had, as one writer remarks, assisted Hitler 'in tearing a further large strip off the Versailles Treaty'.[6] From 1936 to 1939 Germany's outlay on the armed forces accounted for 16.5 per cent of the country's gross national product, twice what Britain and France were spending.

'We have no territorial demands to make in Europe.'
HITLER, 7 MARCH 1936

Germany's next step – reoccupying the demilitarised Rhineland – further emptied the Versailles Treaty and the

Locarno Pact of their credibility, breaching Articles 42 and 43 of the former and Articles 1 and 2 of the latter. Under the Versailles terms Germany had been banned from garrisoning troops or erecting fortifications on the west bank of the Rhine or in a 32-mile strip on the east bank. Germany had endorsed this at Locarno. The final Allied occupation troops had been withdrawn from the area in 1930. On 7 March 1936 – while Hitler was telling the Reichstag he regarded Locarno as void since France had entered into a pact with the Soviet Union – 30,000 German troops marched into the Rhineland, with orders to pull back in the unlikely event of meeting French resistance. Hitler criticised the 'unholy peace treaty of Versailles' but insisted, 'We have no territorial demands to make in Europe. We know that all the tensions which arise from wrong territorial provisions or the disproportion between the sizes of national population and their living room cannot be solved in Europe by war.' He said Germany had no intention of attacking Poland or Czechoslovakia, both of which had alliances with France.[7]

Neither Britain nor France took any action and the League of Nations, acting on a complaint from Belgium and France, was reduced to a motion of condemnation two weeks after the event. Lloyd George – who had played a central part in drafting the Versailles Treaty – considered Germany's action in the Rhineland justified. After a meeting with Hitler in September 1936, Lloyd George described him in an article in the *Daily Express* as a born leader who had no quarrel with Britain and no ambition for hegemony in Europe.

The re-occupation of the Rhineland boosted Hitler's popularity in Germany and provided further confirmation of how limply Britain and France would respond to a determined flouting of Versailles and Locarno. In January 1937, the fourth anniversary of his appointment as chancellor, Hitler announced to the Reichstag that he was revoking the hated Article 231, the war guilt clause, which he said a weak government had been forced to accept.

Although Article 80 of the Versailles Treaty stipulated that there should be no change in Austria's status as an independent country without the consent of the League of Nations, the post-war constitutions of both Germany and Austria had set unification as an ambition. Ebert had referred in 1921 to the Austria *who longingly stretches out her arms to us, as we to her* … A proposed customs union between Germany and Austria had been thwarted by the League of Nations in 1931. No less emotionally than Ebert, Hitler had written in *Mein Kampf* in the 1920s, 'German-Austria must return to the great German mother-country, and not because of any economic considerations … One blood demands one Reich', though he told the Reichstag in May 1935 that Germany had neither the intention nor the desire to annex or incorporate its neighbour. By early 1938 Hitler was placing pressure on the Austrian chancellor, Kurt Schuschnigg, demanding an end to all restrictions on Nazi activity in Austria and the appointment of a Nazi sympathiser, Arthur Seyss-Inquart, to head the security forces. 'You don't believe you can hold me up for half an hour, do you?' Hitler asked Schuschnigg. 'Who knows? Perhaps I'll appear some time overnight in Vienna, like a spring storm.' [8]

On 9 March 1938 Schuschnigg attempted to turn the tables on Hitler by announcing that he would hold a plebiscite on Austrian independence on 13 March. But Austria collapsed in the face of renewed threats, Seyss-Inquart was appointed chancellor, and early on 12 March German troops crossed the border. In the afternoon Hitler drove in triumph through Branau am Inn, his birthplace, where he was greeted by rapturous crowds, then on to Linz. Later that day he signed a 'Law for the Reunion of Austria with the German Reich'. In a plebiscite on 10 April, 99.75 per cent of Austrians supported their incorporation as a province. The new 'Greater Germany', created in defiance of Versailles, established the largest and most powerful state in Europe, increasing the regime's military strength by ten divisions, making the defence of Czechoslovakia impossible. It was to the Sudetenland that Hitler now turned, convinced by the ease with which Austria had fallen that Britain and France posed no threat to his ambitions in central Europe.

The peacemakers at Versailles had shown little interest in the incorporation into Czechoslovakia of over three million German-speakers living in the Sudetenland, though the decision clearly breached Wilson's principle of self-determination. But the Sudetenlanders had been Austrian, not German, citizens before 1918 and Hitler's claim to the area in 1938 went beyond a revision of Versailles. His aim was to destroy Czechoslovakia, one of the few successes among the new states that had emerged from the war. The Sudetenland was the site of many of the country's vital industries and was crucial to its defence. From the spring of 1938 Sudeten Germans, orchestrated by Berlin, complained they were being badly treated by the Czechoslovak authorities. In May German troop movements on the border provoked a partial Czechoslovak mobilisation, prompting the British government to warn Berlin that if France intervened in support of her ally, Britain might feel compelled to follow. But by August Britain was placing pressure on the Czechoslovak government to grant the Sudeten Germans autonomy. A bellicose speech by Hitler on 12 September provoked disturbances in the Sudetenland, leading to British fears that a German attack was imminent.

On 15 September the British prime minister, Neville Chamberlain, flew to Germany to meet Hitler and reached a provisional agreement on self-determination for the Sudetenland. At a second meeting on 22 September Hitler insisted that the area must be transferred to Germany, setting 1 October as the deadline for Czechoslovak troops to withdraw. At a third meeting in Munich on 30 September Chamberlain, Hitler, the French prime minister Daladier and the Italian leader Mussolini agreed that Czechoslovakia should cede the Sudetenland to Germany. Chamberlain described the arrangement as 'peace with honour'. It was, in reality, an attempt to delay what Britain now saw as an inevitable war with Germany. On 15 March 1939 German troops marched into Prague, liquidating what remained of Czechoslovakia and setting up a puppet Slovak state. Germany wound up further unfinished business of Versailles on 22 March by presenting a demand to Lithuania for the return of Memel. Lithuania acquiesced at once.

All that remained was Poland. Germany's grievances over Upper Silesia, Danzig and the Polish Corridor were longstanding. On 31 March 1939, following Germany's destruction of Czechoslovakia, Chamberlain gave an unconditional guarantee of British support to Poland should any European power threaten her independence. Hitler's initial hope had been to tie Poland to Germany by extending a non-aggression treaty the two had signed in 1934. When this failed, he worked to isolate Poland, determined to destroy what remained of Versailles. On 23 August the Soviet Union – having abandoned any hope of an anti-Nazi accord with Britain and France – signed a non-aggression pact with Germany, including an agreement to divide Poland, bringing to fruition General Seeckt's ambition of 1922. Germany invaded Poland on 1

September, provoking Britain and France to declare war on 3 September.

A speech by Hitler to the Reichstag on 6 October offered peace to Britain and France and dwelt on Germany's triumph over Versailles. Poland, the treaty's artificial creation, had been permanently destroyed. 'The Poland of the Versailles Treaty will never rise again.' He said Germany's aims were clear. 'We want to say that we consider the Versailles Treaty extinct, and that the German government, and with it the entire German nation, see no reason and no cause for any further revision except for the demand for such colonial possessions as are due to the Reich and correspond to it.' He warned that if Britain and France chose to continue the conflict, '1918 will never be repeated in German history.'[9]

ooooo

As in 1914, the war initially went well for Germany. Poland fell within weeks under the onslaught of the Wehrmacht. In April 1940 German forces occupied Denmark and Norway, attacking and rapidly overrunning Belgium, the Netherlands, Luxemburg and France in May and June. Hitler forced the French to sign an armistice in the same railway carriage Marshal Foch had used to take Germany's surrender in November 1918. Yugoslavia and Greece fell after a brief campaign in April 1941, while German and Italian armies in North Africa drove the British back into Egypt. On 22 June German troops advanced into the Soviet Union and in December Germany declared war on the United States following the Japanese attack on Pearl Harbor. After three years of triumph the tide began to turn. In July 1942 German and Italian forces were thrown back at El Alamein and in January

1943 Soviet troops destroyed a German army at Stalingrad. Allied troops landed in Normandy on 6 June 1944, beginning an advance towards Germany, while Soviet troops pushed the enemy back into their homeland. Germany unconditionally surrendered on 8 May 1945.

There was to be no grand peace conference, no second Versailles. After much disagreement between the Allies, Germany (and the capital Berlin) was divided into American, British, French and Soviet zones of occupation. The Allies took the step their predecessors had been reluctant or unable to take in 1919 by putting on trial those they considered responsible for conspiring to wage a war of aggression and war crimes. Hitler had committed suicide in April 1945 as Soviet troops entered Berlin, but from November 1945 to October 1946 24 major political and military figures faced an international military tribunal in the Palace of Justice at Nuremberg. Twelve defendants were sentenced to death. There was controversy in Germany and in Allied legal circles over the legitimacy of what some saw as 'victors' justice'. However, the Nuremberg trials ensured the discrediting and destruction of the Nazi leadership and the detailed public exposure of the regime's actions.

By 1949 the occupied zones had frozen into two states, the western capitalist Federal Republic of Germany and the eastern Communist German Democratic Republic. In 1957 West Germany became a founder member of the European Economic Community, and in 1973 both joined the United Nations, the successor to the League of Nations. Forty years after the country's division, after the collapse of the Berlin Wall and of the Communist government in the east, the two parts were to be reunited.

Ebert's widow, Louise, lived in Heidelberg in West Germany

until her death in 1955. The fate of Ebert's son, Friedrich Jr, provides a counterpoint to Ebert's own career. A Socialist like his father, Friedrich Jr was held briefly in a concentration camp by the Nazis. In 1939, at the age of 45, he was called up for military service. In 1946, during the Russian occupation of East Germany, the Socialists were forced to merge with the Communists to form the Socialist Unity Party, reversing the schism of 1918 that had taken place under Ebert. Friedrich Jr became prominent in the new party, serving as mayor of East Berlin from 1948 to 1967 and as chairman of the party faction in the People's Chamber from 1971. In 1973 he was East German acting head of state for a few months, attaining the pinnacle – if only briefly – his father had reached half a century before.

Notes

Preface: *The enemy's revengeful hysteria*

1. Friedrich Stampfer, 'Hour of Heavy Reckoning', in Victor Schiff (trans. Geoffrey Dunlop), *The Germans at Versailles 1919* (Williams & Norgate Ltd, London: 1930) p 70, hereafter Schiff.

2. Alma Luckau, *The German Delegation at the Paris Peace Conference* (Columbia University Press, New York: 1941) p 223, hereafter Luckau, *The German Delegation*.

3. *New York Times Current History*, 10:1:3 (1919: Jun) p 398.

4. Philipp Scheidemann (trans. J E Michell), *Memoirs of a Social Democrat* (2 vols, London: 1929) p 627, hereafter Scheidemann.

5. *New York Times Current History*, 10:2:1 (1919: Jul) p 39.

6. Richard M Watt, *The Kings Depart, The Tragedy of Germany: Versailles and the German Revolution* (Phoenix, London: 2003 paperback ed) p 459, hereafter Watt.

7. Watt, p 477.

8. Alma Luckau, 'Unconditional Acceptance of the Treaty of Versailles by the German Government, June 22–28, 1919', *Journal of Modern History*, Vol 17, No 3 (Sep 1945) p 217, hereafter Luckau, 'Unconditional acceptance'.

9. Luckau, *The German Delegation*, p 481.

1: The Party Man, 1871–1913

1. Harlow James Heneman, *The Growth of Executive Power in Germany, A Study of the German Presidency* (The Voyageur Press, Minneapolis: 1934) p 203, hereafter Heneman.

2. Lucien Laurat, *Marxism and Democracy* (Victor Gollancz, London: 1940) p 53.

3. Giles MacDonogh, *The Last Kaiser, William the Impetuous* (Weidenfeld & Nicolson, London: 2000) p 413, hereafter MacDonogh.

4. Carl E Schorske, *German Social Democracy 1905–1917, The Development of the Great Schism* (Harper & Row, New York: 1955) p 123, hereafter Schorske.

5. Quoted in Richard J Evans, *The Coming of the Third Reich* (Penguin Books, London: 2004) p 8.

6. Scheidemann, p 79.

7. H Tudor and J M Tudor (eds.), *Marxism and Social Democracy: The Revisionist Debate 1896–1898* (Cambridge University Press, Cambridge: 1988) pp 168–9.

8. D K Buse, 'Ebert and the German Crisis, 1917–1920', *Central European History*, 5:3 (Sep 1972) p 245, hereafter Buse, 'German Crisis'.

9. Schorske, pp 123–4; Sebastian Haffner, *Failure of a Revolution. Germany 1918–19* (André Deutsch, London: 1973) p 81, hereafter Haffner.

10. Haffner, p 81.

11. Eric Hobsbawm, 'Confronting Defeat: the German Communist Party', *New Left Review*, 1/61 (May–Jun 1970) p 89.

12. Rosa Luxemburg to Clara Zetkin, 20 March 1907, in Peter Hudis and Kevin B Anderson (eds.), *The Rosa Luxemburg Reader* (Monthly Review Press: New York 2004) p 13.

13. Rosa Luxemburg to Leo Jogiches, 5 January 1899, in Raya Dunayevskaya, *Rosa Luxemburg, Women's Liberation, and Marx's Philosophy of Revolution* (Humanities Press, New Jersey; Harvest Press, Sussex: 1981) p 5.

14. Dieter Groh, 'The "Unpatriotic Socialists" and the State', *Journal of Contemporary History*, Vol 1, No 4 (Oct 1966) p 158.

15. Scheidemann, pp 80, 81–2, 285.

16. Dieter K Buse, 'Party Leadership and Mechanisms of Unity: The Crisis of German Social Democracy Reconsidered, 1910–1914', *Journal of Modern History*, Vol 62, No 3 (Sep 1990) p 491, hereafter Buse, 'Party Leadership'.

17. Quoted in Alex Hall, *Scandal, Sensation and Social Democracy: The SPD Press and Wilhelmine Germany 1890–1914* (Cambridge University Press, Cambridge: 1977) p 124.

18. *The Times*, 22 September 1913.

19. Buse, 'Party Leadership', p 496.

2: The War, 1914–18

1. Hew Strachan, *The First World War, Vol 1: To Arms* (Oxford University Press, Oxford: 2001) pp 35–6, hereafter Strachan.

2. Carlton J H Hayes, 'The History of German Socialism Reconsidered', *American Historical Review*, Vol 23, No 1 (Oct 1917) p 86.

3. *Vorwärts*, 25 July 1914, quoted in John W Mishark, *The Road to Revolution German Marxism and World War 1 – 1914–1919* (Moira Books, Detroit, Michigan: 1967) p 69, hereafter Mishark.

4. Strachan, pp 121–2.

5. Edwyn Bevan, *German Social Democracy during the War* (George Allen and Unwin, London: 1918) p 21, hereafter Bevan.

6. A Joseph Berlau, *The German Social Democratic Party 1914–1921* (Columbia University Press, New York: 1949) p 120, hereafter Berlau.

7. *Elberfeld Freie Presse*, 22 January 1915, quoted in Dieter K Buse, 'Ebert and the Coming of World War 1: A Month from his Diary', *International Review of Social History*, Vol XIII, Part 3 (1968) p 436.

8. 'Rebuilding the International', quoted in Paul Le Blanc (ed.), *Rosa Luxemburg Reflections and Writings* (Humanity Books, Amherst, New York: 1999) p 204.

9. 27 September 1914, quoted in Mishark, p 76.

10. Eric Hobsbawm, *The Age of Empire 1875–1914* (Abacus, London: 2007 paperback ed) p 326.

11. Scheidemann, p 238.

12. Bevan, pp 76, 64.

13. 30 March 1916, in W M Knight-Patterson, *Germany. From Defeat to Conquest 1913–1933* (George Allen and Unwin, London: 1945) p 74, hereafter Knight-Patterson.

14. Mishark, p 117.

15. Scheidemann, p 243.

16. Martin Kettle, *The Silent Dictatorship* (Croom Helm, London: 1976) p 277.

17. Gerald D Feldman, *Army, Industry and Labor in Germany, 1914–1918* (Princeton University Press, Princeton, New Jersey: 1966) p 38.

18. Knight-Patterson, p 92.

19. Scheidemann, p 380.

20. William Carl Matthews, 'The Economic Origins of the Noskepolitik', *Central European History*, 27:1 (1994) p 72.

21. Bevan, p 184.

22. Scheidemann, p 381.

23. Mishark, p 140.

24. Knight-Patterson, p 137.

25. Quoted in *The Times*, 15 December 1924.

26. Buse, 'German Crisis', p 234.

27. Knight-Patterson, p 181.

28. Mishark, p 161.

29. Mishark, p 168.

30. Quoted in Michael Geyer, 'Insurrectionary Warfare: The German Debate about a Levée en Masse in October 1918', *Journal of Modern History*, Vol 73, No 3 (Sep 2001) p 512.

3: Defeat and Revolution, 1918–19

1. Maximilian Alexander Frederick William (trans. W M Calder and C W H Sutton), *The Memoirs of Prince*

Max of Baden (Constable, London: 1928) Vol II, pp 304, hereafter Maximilian.

2. Maximilian, p 312.
3. MacDonogh, p 413.
4. Scheidemann, p 582.
5. Buse, 'German Crisis', p 245.
6. *New York Times Current History*, 9:1:3 (1918: Dec) p 388.
7. Watt, p 200.
8. Buse, 'German Crisis', p 242; Brigid Doherty, 'Figures of the Pseudorevolution', *October*, Vol 84 (Spring 1998) p 68, hereafter Doherty.
9. Jane Caplan, *Government without Administration, State and Civil Service in Weimar and Nazi Germany* (Clarendon Press, Oxford: 1988) p 20.
10. Erzberger was assassinated in August 1921.
11. Herbert Sulzbach, quoted in Max Arthur, *Forgotten Voices of the Great War* (Ebury Press, London: 2003) p 309.
12. Quoted in T E Jessop, *The Treaty of Versailles. Was it Just?* (Thomas Nelson and Sons Ltd, London: 1942) p 95, hereafter Jessop.
13. Quoted in *The Times*, 13 November 1918.
14. Bullitt Lowry, *Armistice 1918* (Kent State University Press, Kent, Ohio: 1996) p 163.
15. Richard N Hunt, 'Friedrich Ebert and the German Revolution in 1918', in Leonard Krieger and Fritz Stern (eds.), *The Responsibility of Power. Historical Essays in Honor of Hajo Holborn* (Doubleday and Company, Garden City, New York: 1967) p 326.
16. Quoted in Heneman, p 208.
17. *The Times*, 12 December 1918.

18. Chris Harman, *The Lost Revolution, Germany 1918 to 1923* (Bookmarks: London: 1997) p 60.

19. Quoted in Holger H Herwig, 'The First Congress of Workers' and Soldiers' Councils and the Problem of Military Reforms', *Central European History*, 1:2 (1968: Jun) p 165

20. Gerald D Feldman, *The Great Disorder Politics, Economics and Society in the German Inflation, 1914–1924* (Oxford University Press, New York and Oxford: 1993) p 123.

21. *The Times*, 7 February 1919.

22. Scheidemann, p 614.

23. *The Times*, 2 March 1925, quoted after his death.

24. *The Times*, 14 February 1919.

25. Knight-Patterson, p 243.

4: Setting the Terms, 1919

1. Ruth Henig, *Versailles and After 1919–1933* (Routledge, 1995: London) p 31, hereafter Henig; Karl Friedrich Nowak (trans. Norman Thomas & E W Dickes), *Versailles* (Victor Gollancz Ltd, London: 1928) p 31, hereafter Nowak.

2. Harold Nicolson, *Peacemaking 1919, being reminiscences of the Paris Peace Conference* (Simon Publications, Safety Harbor, Florida: 2001) p 21, hereafter Nicolson.

3. Speech at Bristol 11 December 1918, *The Times*, 12 December 1918.

4. Quoted in Alan Sharp, *The Versailles Settlement: Peacemaking in Paris, 1919* (Palgrave, London: 1991) p 59.

5. Margaret MacMillan, *Peacemakers. The Paris Conference of 1919 and Its Attempt to End War* (John Murray, London: 2004 paperback ed) p 283, hereafter MacMillan.

6. Quoted in Jessop, p 51.

7. Nicolson, p 95.

8. *The Times*, 7 February 1919.

9. Nowak, p 63.

10. Nowak, pp 121–2.

11. Nowak, p 125.

12. Eberhard Kolb, *The Weimar Republic* (Routledge, London: 2005) p 28.

13. Quoted in MacMillan, p 191.

14. Watt, p 523.

15. Schiff, p 48.

16. Diary entry 1 May 1919, Nicolson, p 321.

17. Herbert Hoover, *The Ordeal of Woodrow Wilson* (McGraw-Hill, New York: 1958) pp 241–2.

18. Luckau, *The German Delegation*, p 222.

19. Jessop, p 55.

20. George Allardice Riddell, *Lord Riddell's Intimate Diary of the Peace Conference and After, 1918–1923* (Victor Gollancz, London: 1933) p 76.

21. Friedrich Stampfer, 'Hour of Heavy Reckoning', in Schiff, p 82.

22. *New York Times Current History*, 10:2:1 (1919: Jul) p 38.

23. Luckau, *The German Delegation*, p 302.

24. Nowak, pp 264–5.

5: Signing the Peace, 1919

1. Knight-Patterson, p 262.

2. Luckau, *The German Delegation*, p 482.
3. *The Times*, 26 June 1919; William Harvey Maehl, *The German Socialist Party: Champion of the First Republic, 1918–1933* (American Philosophical Society, Philadelphia: 1986) pp 45–6.
4. Luckau, 'Unconditional acceptance', p 220.
5. Hermann Müller, 'Signature in the Galerie des Glaces', in Schiff, p 166.
6. There is a full text of the treaty at www.yale.edu/lawweb/avalon/imt/menu.htm
7. Scheidemann, pp 635–6.
8. Diary entry 28 June 1919, Nicolson, p 368.
9. *The Times*, 30 June 1919.
10. Müller, in Schiff, p 171.
11. Müller, in Schiff, pp 169–70.
12. Müller, in Schiff, p 171.
13. *The Times*, 30 June 1919.
14. Sally Marks, *The Illusion of Peace. International Relations in Europe 1918–1933* (MacMillan Education, London: 1976) p 16, hereafter Marks.
15. Kolb, p 33.
16. Richard Bessel, 'Why Did the Weimar Republic Collapse', in Ian Kershaw, *Weimar: Why Did German Democracy Fail?* (Weidenfeld and Nicolson, London: 1990) p 127.
17. *New York Times Current History* 10:2:2 (1919: Aug) p 200.
18. Henig, p 52.
19. MacMillan, p 281.

6: The Brittle Republic, 1919–25

1. *The Times*, 20 February 1919; Scheidemann, p 620.

2. Richard Bessel, *Germany after the First World War* (Clarendon Press, Oxford: 1993) p 222.

3. Count Harry Kessler, quoted in Doherty, p 70.

4. *New York Times Current History*, 11:1:1 (1919: Oct) p 73.

5. Scheidemann, p 642.

6. Gordon A Craig, *The Politics of the Prussian Army 1640–1945* (Clarendon Press, Oxford: 1955) p 377.

7. *The Times*, 19 January 1921.

8. Helmuth Stoecker, *German Imperialism in Africa: From the Beginnings until the Second World War* (C Hurst & Co., London: 1987) p 303.

9. Holger H Herwig, 'Clio Deceived: Patriotic Self-Censorship in Germany after the Great War', *International Security*, Vol 12, No 2 (Autumn 1987) pp 27, 43.

10. *The Times*, 4 March 1921.

11. *The Times*, 9 March 1921.

12. Diary entry 10 November 1923, Viscount d'Abernon, *An Ambassador of Peace*, Vol 2 p 271, cited in Knight-Patterson, p 339.

13. *The Times*, 10 January 1923.

14. Heneman, p 213.

15. William Harvey Maehl, *The German Socialist Party: Champion of the First Republic, 1918–1933* (American Philosophical Society, Philadelphia: 1986) p 93.

16. *The Times*, 12 May 1924.

17. Marks, p 53.

18. Heneman, p 220.

7: The Unravelling of Versailles, 1925–45

1. Peter Fritzsche, 'Presidential Victory and Popular Festivity in Weimar Germany: Hindenburg's 1925 Election', *Central European History*, 23: 2/3 (1990: Jun/Sep) p 205.

2. Marks, p 106.

3. Ian Kershaw, *Hitler 1889–1936: Hubris* (Allen Lane The Penguin Press, London: 1998), p 150, hereafter Kershaw, *Hitler 1889–1936*.

4. Quoted in *The Times*, 29 June 1933.

5. *The Times*, 18 March 1935.

6. Kershaw, *Hitler 1889–1936*, p 558.

7. *The Times*, 9 March 1936.

8. Ian Kershaw, *Hitler 1936–1945: Nemesis* (Allen Lane The Penguin Press, London: 2000), p 70.

9. *The Times*, 7 October 1939.

Chronology

YEAR	AGE	THE LIFE AND THE LAND
1871		Jan: Prussia wins Franco-Prussian War. German Empire proclaimed at Versailles.
		4 Feb: Ebert is born in Heidelberg, the seventh child of Karl and Katharina Ebert.
		May: France cedes Alsace-Lorraine to Germany and pays indemnity.
1872	1	Germany, Austria-Hungary and Russia form Three Emperors' League.
1879	8	Germany forms Dual Alliance with Austria-Hungary.
1882	11	Triple Alliance of Germany, Austria-Hungary and Italy.
1884	13	Congress of Berlin opens way to establishment of German African colonies: Germany occupies South-West Africa.
1885	14	Ebert leaves school to become an apprentice saddlemaker.
		Germany annexes Tanganyika and Zanzibar.

YEAR	HISTORY	CULTURE
1871	Britain annexes Kimberley diamond fields in South Africa.	Lewis Carroll, *Through the Looking Glass*. Charles Darwin, *The Descent of Man*.
1872	Civil war in Spain. Grant re-elected US President.	Thomas Hardy, *Under the Greenwood Tree*. J M Whistler, painting 'The Artist's Mother'.
1879	Zulu War. First London telephone exchange opens.	Henry James, *Daisy Miller*. Tchaikovsky, opera 'Eugen Onegin'.
1882	British occupy Egypt. Hiram Maxim patents his machine gun.	R L Stevenson, *Treasure Island*. Tchaikovsky, '1812 Overture'.
1884	General Gordon arrives in Khartoum. Gold discovered in the Transvaal.	Mark Twain, *Huckleberry Finn*. Seurat, painting 'Une Baignade à Asnières'.
1885	General Gordon killed in fall of Khartoum to the Mahdi. The Congo becomes the personal possession of King Léopold II of Belgium.	Maupassant, *Bel Ami*. H Rider Haggard, *King Solomon's Mines*. Gilbert and Sullivan, operetta 'The Mikado'.

YEAR	AGE	THE LIFE AND THE LAND
1888	17	Ebert completes apprenticeship.
		Wilhelm II becomes Kaiser.
1889	18	Ebert joins saddlemakers' union and socialist party, and travels Germany for work.
1890	19	Wilhelm II dismisses Bismarck.
		Sozialdemokratische Partei Deutschlands – SPD – formed.
1891	20	Ebert moves to Bremen in northern Germany.
		SPD adopts Marxist Erfurt Programme.
1893	22	Ebert marries Louise Rump; becomes an innkeeper.
1894	23	Ebert's first child Friedrich Jr born (four more follow); Ebert elected Bremen SPD chairman.
1896	25	Ebert is delegate to SPD national congress.
		Wilhelm's 'Kruger Telegram' following Jameson Raid in Transvaal raises tension with Britain.

YEAR	HISTORY	CULTURE
1888	Suez Canal convention. 'Jack the Ripper' murders in London.	Rudyard Kipling, *Plain Tales from the Hills*. Van Gogh, painting 'The Yellow Chair'.
1889	Austro-Hungarian Crown Prince Rudolf commits suicide at Mayerling. London Dock Strike.	Jerome K Jerome, *Three Men in a Boat*. Richard Strauss, symphonic poem 'Don Juan'.
1890	First general election in Japan.	Oscar Wilde, *The Picture of Dorian Gray*. Mascagni, opera 'Cavelleria Rusticana'. First moving picture shows in New York.
1891	Franco-Russian entente. Young Turk Movement founded in Vienna.	Thomas Hardy, *Tess of the D'Urbervilles*. Mahler, Symphony No 1.
1893	Franco-Russian alliance signed. Benz constructs his four-wheel car.	Oscar Wilde, *A Woman of No Importance*. Art Nouveau appears in Europe.
1894	Sino-Japanese War. Dreyfus Case begins in France.	G & W Grossmith, *The Diary of a Nobody*. Anthony Hope, *The Prisoner of Zenda*.
1896	Italian army defeated by Abyssinians at Adowa. Kitchener begins reconquest of the Sudan. Klondike Gold Rush.	Chekhov, *The Seagull*. Nobel Prizes established.

YEAR	AGE	THE LIFE AND THE LAND
1898	27	First Navy Law opens German naval expansion to rival Britain.
		Death of Bismarck.
1899	28	Ebert elected SPD member on Bremen council.
1900	29	Ebert appointed Bremen's first paid labour secretary.
		Germany's Second Navy Law.
1901	30	Failed Anglo-German alliance negotiations.
1904	33	Ebert presides over SPD national congress in Bremen.
1905	34	Ebert is elected to SPD executive as secretary.
		Germany's Schlieffen Plan envisages two-front war against France and Russia.
		Crisis over German and French ambitions in Morocco.
1906	35	Ebert takes up party executive post in Berlin.
		Edward VII of England and Kaiser Wilhelm II of Germany meet.

YEAR	HISTORY	CULTURE
1898	Kitchener defeats Mahdists at Omdurman. Spanish-American War. Paris Métro opened.	Thomas Hardy, *Wessex Poems*. Henry James, *The Turn of the Screw*.
1899	Anglo-Egyptian Sudan Convention. Outbreak of Second Boer War. First Peace Conference at the Hague.	Rudyard Kipling, *Stalky and Co*. Elgar, 'Enigma Variations'.
1900	Second Boer War: relief of Mafeking. Assassination of King Umberto I of Italy. Boxer Rising in China.	Freud, *The Interpretation of Dreams*. Joseph Conrad, *Lord Jim*. Anton Chekhov, *Uncle Vanya*.
1901	Death of Queen Victoria: Edward VII becomes King.	Thomas Mann, *Die Buddenbrooks*. Strindberg, *Dances of Death*. Rudyard Kipling, *Kim*.
1904	Entente Cordiale settles British-French colonial differences. Outbreak of Russo-Japanese War.	J M Barrie, *Peter Pan*. Thomas Hardy, *The Dynasts*.
1905	Port Arthur surrenders to Japanese. Revolution in Russia.	E M Forster, *Where Angels Fear to Tread*. Edith Wharton, *House of Mirth*.
1906	Britain grants self-government to Transvaal and Orange River Colonies. San Francisco earthquake.	John Galsworthy, *A Man of Property*. O Henry, *The Four Million*. Invention of first jukebox.

YEAR	AGE	THE LIFE AND THE LAND
1911	40	Ebert declines invitation to stand as SPD co-chairman but receives 102 votes. Agadir Crisis over Morocco.
1912	41	Ebert is elected as Reichstag deputy for Eberfeld-Barmen. Third Navy Law. Abortive conference with Britain over naval rivalry.
1913	42	Ebert elected SPD co-chairman. German army expansion begins.
1914	43	Aug: Germany declares war on Russia and France; Britain declares war on Germany. Ebert votes in Reichstag to support war as a defensive struggle.
1915	44	First World War: German offensives on Eastern Front; defensive campaign on Western Front. Ebert has increasing contacts in government circles; says SPD desires peace with no territorial annexations.

YEAR	HISTORY	CULTURE
1911	US-Japanese and Anglo-Japanese commercial treaties signed. Italy declares war on Turkey.	D H Lawrence, *The White Peacock*. Saki, *The Chronicles of Clovis*.
1912	The Liner *Titanic* sinks; 1,513 die. Montenegro declares war on Turkey. Woodrow Wilson is elected US President.	Alfred Adler, *The Nervous Character*. C G Jung, *The Theory of Psychoanalysis*. Ravel, 'Daphnis and Chloe'.
1913	Second Balkan war breaks out. US Federal Reserve System is established.	Thomas Mann, *Death in Venice*. Marcel Proust, *Du côté de chez Swann*.
1914	Archduke Franz Ferdinand of Austria-Hungary and his wife are assassinated in Sarajevo. Outbreak of First World War: Battles of Mons, the Marne and First Ypres: trench warfare on the Western Front. Russians defeated at Battles of Tannenberg and Masurian Lakes.	James Joyce, *Dubliners*. Theodore Dreiser, *The Titan*. Film: Charlie Chaplin in *Making a Living*.
1915	Gallipoli campaign. Germans sink the British liner *Lusitania*, killing 1,198. Germans execute British nurse Edith Cavell in Brussels for harbouring British prisoners.	Joseph Conrad, *Victory*. John Buchan, *The Thirty-Nine Steps*. Ezra Pound, *Cathay*. Film: *The Birth of a Nation*.

YEAR	AGE	THE LIFE AND THE LAND
1916	45	First World War: German offensive at Verdun against French; battle of Jutland with British navy. Allies reject German peace proposal.
		Ebert supports U-boat warfare; criticises strikes in war industries.
1917	46	First World War:
		Jan: Germany begins unrestricted U-boat campaign.
		Apr: United States declares war on Germany.
		Ebert becomes SPD senior co-chairman.
		Jun: Ebert attends Stockholm socialist conference on war.
		Jul: Ebert supports opposition 'peace resolution' in Reichstag.
1918	47	Jan: President Wilson's Fourteen Points; Ebert joins Berlin strike committee.
		Mar: Treaty of Brest-Litovsk Treaty with Russia. Ebert supports treaty but leads SPD in Reichstag abstention; German offensives on Western Front followed by successful Allied summer offensive.
		Oct: German naval mutiny begins revolution.
		Nov: Wilhelm II abdicates. Ebert becomes Imperial Chancellor and makes pact with army command. Armistice signed with Allies.
		Dec: Ebert tells army it returns undefeated.
1919	48	Jan: Spartacist Rising defeated.
		Feb: Ebert appointed provisional Reich President. 'Weimar Coalition' formed.
		May–Jun: Ebert rejects Versailles Treaty, then agrees Germany must sign.
		Jun: Germany signs Versailles Treaty.

YEAR	HISTORY	CULTURE
1916	US President Woodrow Wilson is re-elected; issues Peace Note to belligerents in European war. Lloyd George becomes British Prime Minister.	James Joyce, *Portrait of an Artist as a Young Man.* Film: *Intolerance.*
1917	February Revolution in Russia. Balfour Declaration favouring the establishment of a national home for the Jewish People in Palestine. Bolshevik revolution in Russia.	P G Wodehouse, *The Man With Two Left Feet.* T S Eliot, *Prufrock and Other Observations.* Film: *Easy Street.*
1918	Romania signs Peace of Bucharest with Germany and Austria-Hungary. Ex-Tsar Nicholas II and family executed.	Gerald Manley Hopkins, *Poems.* Luigi Pirandello, *Six Characters in Search of an Author.*
1919	Benito Mussolini founds fascist movement in Italy. US Senate votes against ratification of Versailles Treaty, leaving the USA outside the League of Nations.	Thomas Hardy, *Collected Poems.* Herman Hesse, *Demian.* George Bernard Shaw, *Heartbreak House.* Film: *The Cabinet of Dr Caligari.*

YEAR	AGE	THE LIFE AND THE LAND
1920	49	Mar: Ebert flees attempted overthrow of government in Kapp Putsch.
		German army suppresses left-wing revolt in Bavaria.
		Adolf Hitler announces his 25-point programme in Munich.
1921	50	Mar: Ebert complains reparations will force Germans to become 'working slaves'.
		May: Allies set reparations payments.
1922	51	Apr: Germany signs Rapallo Treaty with Russia.
		Jun: German foreign minister Rathenau assassinated.
		Dec: Germany declared in default on reparations payments.
1923	52	Jan: Franco-Belgian occupation of Ruhr begins; Ebert urges passive resistance to occupation.
		Germany declares State of Emergency.
		German inflationary crisis.
		Nov: Hitler leads Munich 'Beer Hall *putsch*': Ebert refuses to become dictator to combat the right.
1924	53	Ebert expelled from saddlers' union.
		Apr: Dawes Plan restructures German reparations payments.
		Dec: Court declares Ebert a traitor for participation in 1918 munitions strike.
1925	54	28 Feb: Ebert dies; buried in Heidelberg.
		Apr: Hindenburg elected Reich President.
		Oct: Germany signs Locarno Treaty.

YEAR	HISTORY	CULTURE
1920	League of Nations comes into existence. Bolsheviks win Russian Civil War. Government of Ireland Act passed.	F Scott Fitzgerald, *This Side of Paradise*. Rambert School of Ballet formed.
1921	Irish Free State established. Washington Naval Treaty signed.	D H Lawrence, *Women in Love*. Prokofiev, 'The Love for Three Oranges'.
1922	Chanak crisis. League of Nations council approves British mandate in Palestine.	T S Eliot, *The Waste Land*. James Joyce, *Ulysses*. British Broadcasting Company (later Corporation) (BBC) founded: first radio broadcasts.
1923	Severe earthquake in Japan destroys all of Yokohama and most of Tokyo. British Mandate in Palestine begins.	P G Wodehouse, *The Inimitable Jeeves*. George Gershwin, 'Rhapsody in Blue'.
1924	Death of Lenin. British Labour Party loses general election after *Daily Mail* publishes the Zinoviev Letter.	Noel Coward, *The Vortex*. E M Forster, *A Passage to India*.
1925	In Italy, Mussolini announces that he will take dictatorial powers. Pound Sterling returns to the Gold Standard.	Virginia Woolf, *Mrs Dalloway*. Film: *Battleship Potemkin*.

YEAR	AGE	THE LIFE AND THE LAND
1926		Sep: Germany joins League of Nations.
1929		Jun: Young Plan reduces German reparations payments: Allies agree to evacuate the Rhineland.
1932		Jul: Reparations abandoned at Lausanne Conference.
1933		Jan: Hitler appointed Reich Chancellor.
		Oct: Germany leaves League of Nations and Disarmament Conference.
1935		Jan: Saar returns to German control.
		Mar: Germany begins rearmament.
1936		Mar: Germany reoccupies Rhineland.
		Mussolini proclaims the Rome-Berlin Axis.
1938		Mar: Germany annexes Austria.
		Oct: Germany occupies Sudetenland following Munich Agreement.
1939		Mar: Germany occupies remainder of Czechoslovakia.
		Aug: Germany signs pact with Soviet Union.
		Sep: German attack on Poland opens Second World War.

YEAR	HISTORY	CULTURE
1926	General Strike in Great Britain.	Ernest Hemingway, *The Sun Also Rises.* Film: *The General.*
1929	Fascists win single-party elections in Italy. The Wall Street Crash.	Erich Remarque, *All Quiet on the Western Front.* Museum of Modern Art New York opens.
1932	F D Roosevelt wins US Presidential election in Democrat landslide.	Aldous Huxley, *Brave New World.* Film: *Grand Hotel.*
1933	Japan announces it will leave the League of Nations.	George Orwell, *Down and Out in Paris and London.* Film: *King Kong.*
1935	King George V's Silver Jubilee. League of Nations imposes sanctions against Italy following its invasion of Abyssinia.	T S Eliot, *Murder in the Cathedral.* Ivy Compton-Burnett, *A House and its Head.* Films: *The 39 Steps.*
1936	Abdication Crisis in Great Britain. Outbreak of Spanish Civil War. Roosevelt, Democrat, re-elected president of the USA.	J M Keynes, *General Theory of Employment, Interest and Money.* Berlin Olympics. Films: *Modern Times.*
1938	Japanese puppet government of China at Nanjing.	Graham Greene, *Brighton Rock.* Film: *The Adventures of Robin Hood.*
1939	Italy invades Albania. Spanish Civil War ends as nationalists take Madrid. Japanese-Soviet clashes in Manchuria. Soviets invade Finland.	John Steinbeck, *The Grapes of Wrath.* Film: *Gone with the Wind.*

YEAR	AGE	THE LIFE AND THE LAND
1940		Apr–Jun: Germany occupies Western Europe.
1941		Jun: Germany invades Soviet Union.
		Dec: Germany declares war on United States.
1942		Jul: German and Italian armies defeated in North Africa at El Alamein.
1943		Feb: Germany army defeated at Stalingrad.
		Allies demand unconditional surrender from Germany and Japan at Casablanca Conference.
		Axis forces in North Africa surrender.
1944		Jun: Allied D-Day landings in France.
		Jul: Hitler escapes assassination attempt.
		Dec: German counter-offensive in the Ardennes fails.
1945		May: Germany unconditionally surrenders and is occupied and divided.

YEAR	HISTORY	CULTURE
1940	Italy declares war on France and Britain. Roosevelt is elected for an unprecedented third term as US president.	Eugene O'Neill, *Long Day's Journey into Night*. Film: *The Great Dictator*.
1941	Japanese troops occupy Indochina. Japan attacks Pearl Harbor, invades Philippines.	Bertold Brecht, *Mother Courage and Her Children*. Film: *Citizen Kane*.
1942	Surrender of Singapore to Japanese: Japanese invade Burma. US landings on Guadalcanal turns Japanese tide.	Albert Camus, *The Outsider*. Films: *Casablanca*.
1943	Allied invasion of Sicily and Italy. Italian King dismisses Mussolini: Italy surrenders unconditionally. Tehran Conference: Churchill, Roosevelt and Stalin meet.	Jean-Paul Sartre, *Being and Nothingness*. Rogers and Hammerstein, 'Oklahoma!'. Film: *For Whom the Bell Tolls*.
1944	British and US forces in Italy liberate Rome. Churchill visits Stalin in Moscow. Free French enter Paris. Roosevelt wins fourth term in office.	Terrence Rattigan, *The Winslow Boy*. Tennessee Williams, *The Glass Menagerie*. Film: *Henry V*.
1945	Roosevelt dies and is succeeded by Truman. USA drops atomic bombs on Hiroshima and Nagasaki. Japan surrenders to Allies.	Evelyn Waugh, *Brideshead Revisited*. Film: *Brief Encounter*.

Further Reading

Despite the controversies surrounding Friedrich Ebert's actions in November 1918 and his role as Germany's first democratic head of state, there is still no full-scale biography in English, a mark perhaps of the difficulties in grasping his 'anti-personality'. A long-awaited book by Professor Dieter Buse regrettably remains unpublished, but three of his articles provide useful information: 'Party Leadership and Mechanisms of Unity: The Crisis of German Social Democracy Reconsidered, 1910–1914', *Journal of Modern History*, Vol 62, No 3 (1990), 'Ebert and the German Crisis, 1917–1920', *Central European History*, 5:3 (1972) and 'Ebert and the Coming of World War 1: A Month from his Diary', *International Review of Social History*, Vol XIII, Part 3 (1968).

A relatively old but detailed study, not easily obtainable but nevertheless recommended, is John W Mishark, *The Road to Revolution German Marxism and World War 1 – 1914–1919* (Moira Books, Detroit, Michigan: 1967). Not all the author's judgements have stood the test of time but there is a wealth of information on Ebert's pre-Weimar political trajectory. Kenneth R Calkins, 'The election of Hugo Haase to the co-chairmanship of the SPD and the crisis of pre-war German social democracy', *International Review of Social History*, Vol XIII, Part 2 (1968), is interesting on Ebert's rise in the party. Richard N Hunt, 'Friedrich Ebert and the German Revolution of 1918', in Leonard Krieger and Fritz Stern (eds.), *The Responsibility of Power. Historical Essays in Honor of Hajo Holborn* (Doubleday and Company, Garden City, New York: 1967), is a sharply-focussed analysis with little sympathy for the choices Ebert made at a turning point in German history.

A number of studies of Ebert's party touch on the man himself, among them Gary P Steenson, *"Not One Man! Not One Penny!" German Social Democracy, 1863–1914* (University of Pittsburg Press, Pittsburg: 1981), which is solid and fluently written, A Joseph Berlau, *The German Social Democratic Party 1914–1921* (Columbia University Press, New York: 1949), and Roger Fletcher (ed.), *Bernstein to Brandt, A Short History of German Social Democracy* (Edward Arnold, London: 1987), a useful canter through the main events. Carl E Schorske, *German Social Democracy 1905–1917, The Development of the Great Schism* (Harper & Row, New York: 1955), is excellent on divisions within the SPD and gives Ebert scant approval. H Tudor and J M Tudor (eds.), *Marxism and Social Democracy: The Revisionist Debate 1896–1898* (Cambridge University Press, Cambridge: 1988) is a superb examination of the arguments between reformists and would-be revolutionary socialists in Ebert's party. Stefan Berger, *The British Labour Party and the German Social Democrats, 1900–1931* (Clarendon Press, Oxford: 1994) is an interesting comparative study. Alex Hall, *Scandal, Sensation and Social Democracy: The SPD Press and Wilhelmine Germany 1890–1914* (Cambridge University Press, Cambridge: 1977) is entertaining and enlightening. David W Morgan, *The Socialist Left and the*

German Revolution: A History of the German Independent Social Democratic Party, 1917–1922 (Cornell University Press, Ithaca and London: 1975) examines the party that split from Ebert's SPD under the pressure of war.

The literature on the First World War is limitless. A relatively recent short but authoritative contribution is Hew Strachan, *The First World War: A New Illustrated History* (Simon and Schuster, London: 2003). The notes are a helpful guide to further reading. Nicholas Stargardt, *The German Idea of Militarism, Radical and Socialist Critics 1866–1914* (Cambridge University Press, Cambridge: 1994), is good for the contrast between the SPD's pre-war anti-militarist assumptions and its actions in 1914. Gerald D Feldman, *Army, Industry and Labor in Germany, 1914–1918* (Princeton University Press, Princeton, New Jersey: 1966) provides a detailed analysis of the impact on wartime moves towards a planned economy that placed socialists in an interesting dilemma. The same writer's *The Great Disorder Politics, Economics and Society in the German Inflation, 1914–1924* (Oxford University Press, New York and Oxford: 1993) is monumental and indispensable for an understanding of the period. Edwyn Bevan, *German Social Democracy during the War* (George Allen and Unwin, London: 1918), stands up well in its judgements of the actions of Ebert and his fellow socialists.

Pierre Broué (eds. Ian Birchall and Brian Pearce, trans. John Archer), *The German Revolution, 1917–1923* (Brill, Boston, Mass.: 2005) would be difficult to better. Among older but still useful studies are A J Ryder, *The German Revolution of 1918: A Study of German Socialism in War and Revolt* (Cambridge University Press, Cambridge & New York: 1967), F L Carsten, *Revolution in Central Europe 1918–1919* (Temple Smith, London: 1972), and Sebastian Haffner, *Failure of a*

Revolution: Germany 1918–19 (Andre Deutsch, London: 1973). Chris Harman, *The Lost Revolution, Germany 1918 to 1923* (Bookmarks: London: 1997) is a brisk account and Richard M Watt provides a readable narrative of the collapse of Imperial Germany and the peace treaty in *The Kings Depart, The Tragedy of Germany: Versailles and the German Revolution* (Phoenix, London: 2003 paperback ed).

For the Treaty of Versailles, see Ruth Henig, *Versailles and After 1919–1933* (Routledge, London: 1995), a short and sharp analysis of the events and historians' views. Alan Sharp, *The Versailles Settlement: Peacemaking in Paris, 1919* (Palgrave, London: 1991) is also a valuable overview. Margaret MacMillan, *Peacemakers The Paris Conference of 1919 and Its Attempt to End War* (John Murray, London: 2004 paperback ed.) is long but readable. M Boemeke, G D Feldman and E Glaser (eds.), *The Treaty of Versailles: A Reassessment after 75 Years* (Cambridge University Press, Cambridge: 1998) provides a useful summing-up. Harold Nicolson, *Peacemaking 1919, being reminiscences of the Paris Peace Conference* (Simon Publications, Safety Harbor, Florida: 2001) remains an interesting personal anti-treaty memoir. See also David Andelman, *A Shattered Peace: Versailles 1919 and the Price We Pay Today* (John Wiley & Sons, New York: 2007).

Studies of what followed the 1918 revolution and Versailles include Eric D Weitz's *Weimar Germany: Promise and Tragedy* (Princeton University Press, Princeton and Oxford: 2007), an evocative study of Weimar politics and culture, Eberhard Kolb, *The Weimar Republic* (Routledge, London: 2005) and Ruth Henig, *The Weimar Republic 1919–1933* (Routledge, London: 1998). On Ebert's party during Weimar, see William Harvey Maehl, *The German Socialist Party: Champion of the First Republic, 1918–1933* (American Philosophical Society,

Philadelphia: 1986). Ian Kershaw, *Weimar: Why Did German Democracy Fail?* (Weidenfeld and Nicolson, London: 1990) is an informative collection of essays on the Republic's collapse. Richard J Evans, *The Coming of the Third Reich* (Penguin Books paperback, London: 2003) cannot be rivalled for its account of the descent into Nazi rule.

Picture Sources

The author and publishers wish to express their thanks to the following sources of illustrative material and/or permission to reproduce it. They will make proper acknowledgements in future editions in the event that any omissions have occurred.

Corbis: p. vi; all other pictures private collections or public domain.

Endpapers
The Signing of Peace in the Hall of Mirrors, Versailles, 28th June 1919 by Sir William Orpen (Bridgeman Art Library)
Front row: Dr Johannes Bell (Germany) signing with Herr Hermann Müller leaning over him
Middle row (seated, left to right): General Tasker H Bliss, Col E M House, Mr Henry White, Mr Robert Lansing, President Woodrow Wilson (United States); M Georges Clemenceau (France); Mr David Lloyd George, Mr Andrew Bonar Law, Mr Arthur J Balfour, Viscount Milner, Mr G N Barnes (Great Britain); Prince Saionji (Japan)
Back row (left to right): M Eleftherios Venizelos (Greece);

Dr Afonso Costa (Portugal); Lord Riddell (British Press);
Sir George E Foster (Canada); M Nikola Pašić (Serbia);
M Stephen Pichon (France); Col Sir Maurice Hankey,
Mr Edwin S Montagu (Great Britain); the Maharajah of
Bikaner (India); Signor Vittorio Emanuele Orlando (Italy);
M Paul Hymans (Belgium); General Louis Botha (South
Africa); Mr W M Hughes (Australia)

Jacket images

(Front): Private collection.
(Back): *Peace Conference at the Quai d'Orsay* by Sir
William Orpen (akg Images).
Left to right (seated): Signor Orlando (Italy); Mr Robert
Lansing, President Woodrow Wilson (United States); M
Georges Clemenceau (France); Mr David Lloyd George, Mr
Andrew Bonar Law, Mr Arthur J Balfour (Great Britain);
Left to right (standing): M Paul Hymans (Belgium); Mr
Eleftherios Venizelos (Greece); The Emir Feisal (The
Hashemite Kingdom); Mr W F Massey (New Zealand);
General Jan Smuts (South Africa); Col E M House (United
States); General Louis Botha (South Africa); Prince Saionji
(Japan); Mr W M Hughes (Australia); Sir Robert Borden
(Canada); Mr G N Barnes (Great Britain); M Ignacy
Paderewski (Poland)

Index

Makers of the Modern World

UK PUBLICATION: November 2008 to December 2010
CLASSIFICATION: Biography/History/
    International Relations
FORMAT: 198 × 128mm
EXTENT: 208pp
ILLUSTRATIONS: 6 photographs plus 4 maps
TERRITORY: world

Chronology of life in context, full index, bibliography innovative layout with sidebars